Uniforms of the Peninsular War

in Colour
1807–1814

By the same author

Uniforms of Waterloo
Uniforms of the American Civil War
World Uniforms and Battles 1815–50
Uniforms of the Retreat from Moscow 1812

Philip J. Haythornthwaite

Uniforms of the Peninsular War
in Colour
1807–1814

Illustrated by
Michael Chappell

'*My Flint is Sharpe,
My Powdre Dry,
If Boney comes,
I'll Make him DYE*'

BLANDFORD PRESS
Poole   Dorset

Blandford Press Ltd,
Link House, West Street,
Poole, Dorset BH15 1LL

First published 1978
Copyright © 1978 Blandford Press Ltd

All rights reserved. No part of this book may be reproduced, or transmitted in any form or by any means, electronic or mechanical, including photocopying, recording or by any information storage and retrieval system, without permission in writing from the Publisher.

Filmset in Great Britain by
Northumberland Press Ltd, Gateshead,
Tyne and Wear
Printed and bound by
Richard Clay (The Chaucer Press) Ltd,
Bungay, Suffolk
Colour plates by
Sackville Press, Billericay

ISBN 0 7137 0841 7

CONTENTS

Historical Introduction to the Peninsular War	1
Armies of the Peninsular War	11
Britain and France	11
Spain	13
Portugal	15
The French Allies	17
Uniforms of the Peninsular War	18
Equipment and Campaign Kit	24
Shoes	26
Colour Plates	29
Colour Plate Descriptions	93
Black and White Plates	152
Black and White Plate Descriptions	158
Appendix I – British Infantry Regiments in the Peninsula	161
Appendix II – Orders of Battle	163
Appendix III – The Battle of Talavera	171
Bibliography	175

AUTHOR'S NOTE

As this book is concerned with the uniforms of the Peninsular War, the oft-catalogued events of the campaign are covered only briefly in the Historical Introduction. Notes on the organization and characteristics of the various armies are not comprehensive and concentrate on details peculiar to the Peninsular War.

Contemporary and modern spelling of place-names are often at variance; thus can be found Fuentes de Oñoro, Fuentes d'Onor and (in official documents) Fuentes Onova; Rolica and Roleia; Bussaco, Busaco and Busac; Badajoz, Badajos and even Badahoo.

Of the many works cited in the bibliography, the most accessible are the other titles in the Blandford Press Colour Series. To facilitate initial further reading, the text in places contains precise references to illustrations in other volumes of the Blandford series.

HISTORICAL INTRODUCTION TO THE PENINSULAR WAR

At the end of 1807, only Britain stood between Napoleon Bonaparte, Emperor of the French, and the domination of western and central Europe. Napoleon attempted to counter this threat by the 'Continental System' – the prohibition of British goods in Europe. As only Portugal refused to join the anti-British blockade, Napoleon determined to force them into submission, a task which depended upon his Spanish allies allowing the passage of a French army, through the Iberian Peninsula (hence the name of the war).

Spain, nominally ruled by the inept King Charles IV, was actually controlled by the Queen's favourite minister, Godoy, an unscrupulous adventurer whose power had reduced Spain (and her army) to a state of total inefficiency and corruption. The King, Godoy and the heir-apparent Prince Ferdinand hated one another and thus presented no common face against Napoleon, who sent General Junot with 30,000 men through Spain and into Portugal, occupying Lisbon in December 1807; the Portuguese Royal Family fled to Brazil. With the best Spanish troops – General La Romana's 15,000 men – contracted to fight for the French in Northern Europe, 100,000 more French marched unopposed into Spain. However, civil disorder followed, Godoy was overthrown and Charles IV abdicated in favour of his son. In defiance of the virtual annexation of their country, a popular uprising in Madrid murdered some 130 French troops (2 May 1808); brutal reprisals massacred scores. With Ferdinand interned in France, pro-French factions 'requested' that Napoleon's brother Joseph should be 'elected' King, which he was proclaimed in June. The outraged Spanish people turned the treacherous Ferdinand into a martyr as revolt flared and forces were raised by regional 'juntas' with no co-ordination nor any common aim save the desire to drive the French from their country.

The Spanish were singularly ill-fitted to oppose Napoleon. The army – even after the return of La Romana and many of his troops, taken home by British transports – was in a wretched condition, years of neglect and theft of funds reducing them to a disorganized body of ragged, starving troops, indolent and worthless officers and totally incompetent leaders. In addition, the Bonapartist faction had considerable support from those favouring Joseph's liberal ideas and fearing popular revolt for any reason. Consequently, the field army – a struggling, inefficient rabble lacking transport, equipment and pitifully short of cavalry horses – usually disgraced itself: hardly surprising, given woeful leadership and a medieval attitude to war. The irregular bands of patriots (and bandits) fighting a guerrilla war, however, were another matter entirely.

The terrain was against the French; impassable mountains with ideal ambush-points, 'roads' of dust in summer and mud in winter, freezing nights and burning days, snowbound passes and land so poor that the peasants were at subsistence level, meant that the French had to drag their lines of communication over the Pyrenees and use thousands of troops to keep them open.

Marshal Murat, Napoleon's original vice-regent in Spain, relinquished command and Napoleon, directing operations from Bayonne, despatched forces to crush the 'juntas'. Success was mixed: General Merle routed the Spanish Army of Estramadura at Cabezon, defeating the corrupt and hopeless General Cuesta, but Marshal Moncey's expedition was repelled from Valencia, whilst the citizens of Saragossa with a few regulars heroically defied the French General Lefebvre-Desnöettes' attempts to capture their city. In July 1808 Cuesta forcibly took command of the army of the Galician 'junta' and was predictably routed at Medina del Rio Seco (14 July). Nine days later, however, General Dupont with an isolated force of 17,500 French surrendered to Andalusian troops at Baylen; those prisoners not massacred were left to rot in Spanish prison-hulks. It was a shattering blow to the French and, as reinforcements could not be rushed forward in time, King Joseph evacuated Madrid and withdrew north, beyond the River Ebro.

This left Junot isolated in Portugal, where despite unrest there was no open opposition until August 1808, when a 15,000-strong British expedition was landed, commanded by Sir Arthur Wellesley, a young general with a spectacular record in India and Denmark. British intervention was not surprising, as any nation opposed to Napoleon could expect British subsidy and, as in Portugal's case, military assistance. On 17 August Wellesley won a minor victory at Rolica and repelled Junot's assault at Vimiero four days later. Immediately after Vimiero, the arrival of two senior (and elderly) British generals – Sir Harry Burrard and Sir Hew Dalrymple – took over-all command from Wellesley. Not realizing Junot's desperate position, Dalrymple arranged the Convention of

Cintra, by which Junot's forces were evacuated, keeping their arms, in British ships. This 'liberation' of Portugal provoked such vehement public indignation in Britain that the three British generals were called home to explain what the cartoonist Woodward termed 'The Convention that Nobody owns, that saved old Junot's Baggage and Bones'. Only Wellesley was exonerated from having assisted the escape of a defeated enemy.

Meanwhile, the 30,000 British troops in Portugal fell to the command of Sir John Moore, whose reform of infantry tactics and light infantry training was to play a great part in British success in the war. In September 1808 he was ordered to take 20,000 men into Spain, supported by 15,000 more under Sir David Baird, to co-operate with the Spanish 'juntas', whose forces were still unco-ordinated, ill-disciplined, badly-led and whose leaders were unwilling to assist Moore and incapable of grasping the true situation. As Moore's troops dragged themselves over abysmal roads towards Salamanca, Napoleon rushed forward over 80,000 troops and took personal command. Realizing himself alone against the entire French force, Moore ordered a withdrawal until his political masters pointed out that a retreat would damage Anglo-Spanish relations. Moore's brave second advance decided the outcome of the war, or so Napier considered; it forced Napoleon to turn against him rather than administering the *coup de grâce* to the Spanish, and enabled the defences of Portugal to be prepared; otherwise, Napoleon could have captured the British base, Lisbon.

Moore hoped to catch the French army of Marshal Soult before it could be reinforced by Junot, but despite a sharp cavalry success at Sahagun, the combined Moore–Baird army learnt of the fall of Madrid (4 December) and realized that no help could be expected from the Spanish. Pursued by Napoleon, Moore began a horrendous withdrawal to Corunna, through ice and snow, over impossible roads; discipline in the disheartened British army broke down completely, and although the starving army always re-formed when a rearguard action was required, the retreat became a staggering rabble which committed excesses of pillage and drunkenness (for example the rearguard was forced to abandon 1,000 men lying drunk in the village of Bembibre; most were slaughtered by the French vanguard). The road was strewn with frozen corpses, including many camp-followers, soldiers' wives and children, until the evacuation-points of Corunna and Vigo were reached. Even then, the shattered army had to repel an attack at Corunna before embarkation, in which Moore was slain. Commissary Schaumann described the 'victors': 'They were all in tatters, hollow eyed, and covered with blood and filth. They looked so terrible that the people made the sign of the cross as they passed ...' Despite the retreat, the exertions of a few, like Sergeant Newman of the 43rd Light Infantry who collected about a hundred stragglers and held a village in a heroic rearguard action, set the pattern for the invincible army which was to serve under Wellesley.

Two more Spanish defeats in January and February 1809 were followed on 20 February by the fall of Saragossa after a terrible siege in which only 20,000 of the 54,000 Spaniards killed were soldiers, the civilians fighting a bloody street-battle until, starved and disease-ridden, they capitulated. The real character of the Spanish people was shown by the actions of folk-heroes like 'the Maid of Saragossa' who crewed a cannon around which lay the corpses of her family, not by the idiot generals and their capering 'armies'.

Britain decided to continue the war in support of her Portuguese allies for two reasons: the assurance by Wellesley that he could hold Portugal with 20,000 British and a re-organized Portuguese army, and the fact that Spain was so large and its population so hostile that the French could never hold it in complete subjugation. Given over-stretched lines of communication, inadequate supply and vigorous guerrilla activity, the French position was hopeless from the beginning. With the Portuguese army re-constructed by British General Sir William Beresford, and a remarkable network of strongpoints (the lines of Torres Vedras) constructed to protect Lisbon, Wellesley had a secure base from which to defend Portugal and ultimately advance into Spain. By integrating British and Portuguese regiments into a system of divisions, Wellesley forged what has been called (with the possible exception of the B.E.F. of 1914) the finest army ever fielded by Britain.

Cuesta continued to be a greater danger to his allies than his enemies when he was defeated yet again at Medellin (28 March 1809), but on 12 May Wellesley chased Soult out of Oporto and over the frontier into Spain. Harried by guerrillas and the remnants of La Romana's Spanish, the French abandoned Galicia. Wellesley took the offensive with Cuesta, who again disgraced himself and allowed the French to attack Wellesley with the combined forces of King Joseph and Marshal Victor. Four Spanish battalions fired an initial volley and, terrified by the noise of their own muskets, bolted; the British, however, stood firm and beat off – just – repeated French attacks at Talavera (28 July 1809) and the French withdrew. Though a case of the usual superiority of the British line formation against the unwieldy French attack in column, victory had not been easy and Wellesley had still to perfect his army into the smooth-running machine it became. But Talavera raised Allied morale and earned the title of Viscount Wellington for the British commander.

Though reinforced by Craufurd's Light Brigade, after a remarkable forced march, Wellington went on to the defensive; fortunately so, for on 19 November General Areizago's 52,000 Spanish were routed, and in December the eight-month siege of Gerona ended with a capitulation to the French. By January 1810 there were 325,000 French in Spain (including some 'foreign' contingents of mixed value), with Marshal Masséna instructed to capture Portugal. The border fortresses of Ciudad Rodrigo and Almeida fell to the French (the latter when the magazine accidentally exploded) but Wellington halted the French at Busaco (27 September 1810), an action in which the re-organized Portuguese performed with credit, and then retired behind the Lines of Torres Vedras, so skilfully designed that they could be held by only 2,500 British troops, 25,000 Portuguese militia and La Romana's 8,000 Spaniards. Masséna settled down in front of the Lines.

In southern Spain, the French laid siege to Cadiz, the capital of 'free' Spain, in February 1810; reinforced by 8,000 British, it held successfully. Marshal Soult solidified French control of Andalusia but could offer little help to Masséna, starved by a Portuguese 'scorched earth' policy and harried by partisans. As he withdrew in March 1811 the frontier outpost of Badajos surrendered to the French, but this success was counter-balanced by a swift thrust from Cadiz by Sir Thomas Graham's Anglo-Spanish army, inflicting a sharp reverse on the French at Barrossa (5 March 1811). Re-equipped and reinforced, Masséna returned to relieve the beleaguered French garrison in Almeida, but met Wellington at Fuentes de Oñoro (5 May). Both sides suffered heavily in a brutal street-fight centred in the village until Masséna withdrew, the French garrison of Almeida escaping with him.

Meanwhile, Marshal Soult marched to relieve Badajos, besieged by Beresford's wing of Wellington's army. Beresford met the French at Albuera (16 May 1811), a Spanish division heroically holding the French until the Anglo-Portuguese came up. The first British brigade into action (Colborne's) was caught by French cavalry and Polish lancers before it could form square (the universal formation for defence against cavalry), losing no less than 1361 men out of a total of 2066 in a matter of moments. The other British units stood their ground and both sides poured shot into each other for almost an hour, sometimes at only twenty yards range, the British 'dying hard' as exhorted by Col. Inglis of the 57th. When the carnage ended with a French withdrawal, almost 6,000 Allied and probably 8,000 French had fallen, the most appalling slaughter of the war, in which the steadfast behaviour of the British infantry passed into legend.

Neither side attempted any audacious manoeuvre for the remainder of the year; Marshal Marmont replaced Masséna and a series of indecisive actions culminated in the defeat of General Girard's French force by the British General Hill at Arroyo dos Molinos (4 November 1811), which provided one of the humorous vignettes of the war: as the British surprise attack poured into the village, Girard was observed gnashing his teeth and leaping on his cocked hat in anger at being taken by surprise!

Before describing the decisive year of 1812, the two vastly different wars waged in the Peninsula should be noted. When not actually engaged in battle, there was much fraternization between the British and French, taken to such proportions as dining in each other's messes, the barter of food, alcohol, tobacco and even clothing, unofficial truces between outposts, the treatment of enemy wounded and mutual cessation of firing to enable casualties to be removed. Attitudes of British and French to each other seem strange to twentieth-century eyes, the British Colonel Vivian for example writing 'we now ride along side by side, within five yards of each other, without any more danger of being shot than you are when hunting on the town burrows. This is doing as gentlemen should. They really are devilish civil, honourable fellows, and know how to make war . . .' One French general even had a regular delivery of London newspapers from the British lines in order to follow the fortunes of his investments in British government stock! Whilst we may sympathize with the French officer mentioned by Parquin as unwilling to fight the British after having taken refuge in England during the French Revolution, it is with difficulty that modern eyes can reconcile Col. George Napier's statement: 'I should hate to fight out of personal malice or revenge, but have no objection to fight for Fun and Glory.'

Quite different was the guerrilla war waged against the French, who throughout the war had to fight on two fronts – against the Allied field armies and against the Spanish (and Portuguese) guerrillas in their rear. Led by patriots, bandit-chiefs or sometimes maniac killers, Spanish guerrilla bands sometimes several thousand strong constantly cut communications, massacred small detachments, assassinated sentries and intercepted couriers; the French vainly tried to suppress such activities by counter-atrocity, as portrayed in Goya's 'Disasters of War'. Every conceivable torture and outrage was committed by both sides, including the slaughter of unarmed civilians and camp-followers – and it provided an excuse for pillage, banditry and vendetta under the guise of patriotism. One estimate puts the French loss to guerrillas throughout the war at a hundred men *per day*, but figures alone cannot convey the horror. Parquin mentions a chieftain operating under the famous 'El Empecinado' (Juan Martin Diaz, a guerrilla 'general' who later entered politics and ended on the gallows), an unfrocked priest who systematically hanged any man and disembowelled any woman who fell into his hands. Even a hard-bitten veteran like Capt. Charles François (not above murder himself) wrote with horror about what he saw – a French general, his wife and child sawn in half – a captured French hospital containing 400 murdered patients and 53 buried alive – and the discovery of an insane Frenchman, the sole survivor of a massacre of 1,200 unarmed invalids. A typical example of French retaliation is provided by Barrès: in March 1810 a party of French grenadiers and a female *cantinière* (sutleress) fell behind a column of march and were found next day, their throats cut, 'with refinements of cruelty'. The battalion commander marched to the village responsible, lined up all the inhabitants, razed every building and began to shoot the villagers until the guilty men confessed. Four innocent people were killed before the fifth disclosed the culprits, who were instantly slain. By no means was the Peninsular War 'doing as gentlemen should' . . .

With French strength sapped by the recall of troops to fight in Europe, Wellington took the offensive, storming Ciudad Rodrigo (19 January 1812), at the cost of the Light Division's dynamic leader, 'Black Bob' Craufurd, slain in the breach of the fortress wall. Hampered by a ramshackle Portuguese siege-train Wellington pressed on to Badajos, the second vital frontier post. Thousands died in the inferno of a barricaded breach in the defences before a secondary attack scaled the walls at the rear (6 April 1812), almost 30 per cent. of the attackers falling before the French capitulated. Shell-shocked by the appalling carnage at the breach, a huge mob of drunken British soldiers rampaged through the city, completely out of control. The captured French Governor Philippon and his two daughters only escaped death by their escort of British officers slashing at their own men to clear a path from the ravaged city. After two days the men were brought under control by fresh troops and the threat of a gallows; there was little repetition of the disgraceful (but perhaps explicable) scenes of Badajos.

Wellington advanced into Spain, cutting communications between the armies of Marmont and Soult. For more than a month Wellington and Marmont manoeuvred in close proximity, neither able to gain an advantage of terrain or opportunity. At Salamanca (22 July 1812) Wellington saw his chance when Marmont strung out his army in a four-mile line. Spear-headed by a swift cavalry charge, Wellington smashed the French who suffered some 14,000 casualties to the Allies' 5,000+. Wellington, previously known as a 'defensive general', had won a major victory by manoeuvre and in August occupied an ecstatic Madrid; but advancing in an attempt to capture Burgos with insufficient siege equipment he was ultimately compelled to retire in the face of converging French armies. A harrowing retreat – though nothing like that to Corunna – cost the British 3,000 men, but when the campaigning season ended Spain south of the Tagus was free, the French were suffering from ever-increasing guerrilla activity, and the disasters which had befallen Napoleon's 'Grande Armée' in Russia not only deprived the army in Spain of reinforcements but actually drew seasoned troops from the Peninsula.

A 'sideshow' was conducted on the coast of eastern Spain, an ineffective expedition of Anglo-Spanish troops with some Italians and British 'foreign corps', led by the inefficient Sir John Murray (later court-martialled) and planned by Lord William Bentinck, 'not right-headed'. Despite a minor victory at Castalla and the half-capture of Tarragona, the expedition was a failure in all but one respect: as with guerrilla activity, the threat of amphibious operations occupied Marshall Suchet's French occupation forces which could have been better-employed elsewhere.

Wellington advanced rapidly in 1813, brilliantly outflanking the main French defensive line and causing the final abandonment of Madrid by King Joseph in May. Advancing in three columns Wellington gave the French no respite, until in June Joseph and Marshal Jourdan decided to make a stand at Vittoria. Expecting a frontal attack, the French collapsed as Wellington turned both flanks and split the centre (21 June); despite a determined stand by elements of the French army and a poor Allied pursuit, Vittoria was the decisive battle of the war. Although the French lost only about 8,000 of their 66,000 men, Wellington captured 143 out of 150 guns, plus acres of baggage and Joseph's treasury, and most of the French army became a disorganized rabble. One reason for the lack of determined pursuit was that for several hours thousands of Allied troops ransacked the abandoned baggage, appropriating cash and valuables worth literally millions in sterling.

Besieging the remaining border-fortresses of San Sebastian and Pamplona, Wellington wisely declined to invade France as Marshal Soult returned to over-all command of the remaining French armies. Soult counter-attacked in an attempt to reach the besieged garrisons, inept British subordinate commanders allowing the French to force the passes of Roncevalles and Maya despite heroic resistance by outnumbered British. In several days of heavy fighting in the Battle of the Pyrenees, Soult's attack faltered and Wellington's counterattack drove the French back with about 13,000 casualties to some 7,000 Allied, despite initial overwhelming numerical superiority of the French. San Sebastian was stormed on 31 August, with some looting and pillage after its fall; the same day saw Soult's last attack, driven off without difficulty by the steadfast conduct of a Spanish division. Despite confused political wrangling by the Spanish (and Portuguese) Wellington forced a way across the Bidassoa in early October. France was invaded.

Though Pamplona was still in French hands and Suchet was still holding out in Spain, Allied victory was already assured. In December 1813 Napoleon wrote: 'I do not want Spain either to keep or to give away. I will have nothing more to do with that country ...' The defence of France was another matter, but Wellington pushed on, crossing the River Nivelle after the fall of Pamplona (25 October 1813). By preventing plundering and ill-treatment of the French civilian population by his army, Wellington ensured that there would be no French version of the Spanish guerrilla war; indeed, by 1814 the Allied army was receiving better co-operation from the French civilians than was Soult!

Soult continued to retire with skill, suffering defeat at Orthez (27 February 1814) before taking up a position at Toulouse, where (it was believed) Suchet might strike north and attempt to join Soult. Wellington attacked first (10 April), capturing the city at heavy cost, but Soult escaped on the 11th. News of Napoleon's abdication arrived on the following day; the Peninsular War was over.

The hard-fought war provided untarnishable laurels for the British army, but what was its significance in the wider aspect of the Napoleonic Wars as a whole? Napoleon called the Peninsular campaigns his 'Spanish ulcer', an unrelieved drain on men and *matériel*. The very nature of his task – to subjugate a large country with difficult terrain, determined inhabitants and a limited number of troops both ill-supplied and badly-led – pointed towards eventual defeat. Lack of co-operation between French commanders and the presence of a comparatively well-supplied, professional British army led by the greatest general produced by Britain, set the seal not only on French defeat in the Iberian Peninsula, but on the Napoleonic Wars as a whole. Had he not meddled in Spanish and Portuguese affairs, Napoleon might never have been overthrown.

Portugal suffered severely during the war; Spain was utterly devastated. When Ferdinand VII finally ascended his throne he proved himself a tyrant of the first degree, laying the foundations for rebellion and civil war which tore the country apart on several occasions in future years. For a final comment on the Peninsular War, the following was often scrawled upon walls by disenchanted French soldiers, watching their leaders strip the country of its valuables while they themselves starved:

'This war in Spain means death for the men, ruin for the officers, a fortune for the generals!'

In the event, it ruined not only the generals but an Emperor as well.

ARMIES OF THE PENINSULAR WAR

Britain and France

The details below are necessarily brief, most attention being paid to formations peculiar to the Peninsular War.

The basic organization of any infantry battalion was similar for all armies. A number of 'centre' or 'battalion' companies (ranging in number from the eight of a British battalion 'establishment' to the seven, later four, of a French) were complemented by one or two 'élite' companies, usually one of grenadiers (in theory the largest and bravest veterans in the battalion) and one of light infantry ('voltigeurs' – vaulters – in the French), being the most agile men, trained to act in open order as fast-moving skirmishers to precede attacks, delay pursuers and provide the army's protective 'screen'. In practice the difference between élite and ordinary companies was often negligible in all save *esprit de corps*. Certain units – for example those comprising the British Light Division – were composed wholly of light infantry, though the French 'light infantry' in practice was little different from the line. 'Riflemen' – light infantry armed with accurate rifled muskets and always operating in 'open order' – were restricted to the British army. Composite battalions were sometimes formed from the combined élite companies of a division, either grenadiers acting as a veteran reserve or light companies forming extra light infantry battalions; the latter were favoured by the British, the former by the French.

Cavalry regiments were organized into squadrons, each comprising a number of troops or companies; the senior company in the French army was 'élite', the counterpart of the infantry grenadiers, a practice not used by the British. The strength of artillery batteries varied, usually six or eight guns including at least one howitzer per battery (or troop of horse artillery).

Several battalions formed a brigade, in the French case sometimes comprising different battalions of the same regiment. Several brigades formed a division (only introduced into British service after Wellington's re-organization), often a self-sufficient entity complete with light troops and artillery.

Regimental establishments existed only on paper, strengths on campaign varying widely; for example a British infantry battalion. The 1st Battn of a two-battalion regiment, when ordered on service, officially consisted of ten companies of 100 men each, the less-effective personnel being exchanged with the junior battalion, the total strength including officers being around 1,100. The junior battalion when ordered on service would have to leave behind the less effective men from both, giving a strength of around 700. Single-battalion regiments also often fielded 700, though Foot Guards battalions had more, usually 1,200, and even on campaign seldom less than 800. The theoretical establishment rarely applied on campaign, strengths of 1,000 being very rare (for example the 1/4th at Busaco and the 1/42nd at Salamanca). Actual strengths were much less; at the end of 1811 only nine of Wellington's forty-six battalions (including Guards) had more than 700, with eleven under 400; the strongest (1/43rd) had 1,005 and the weakest (2/38th) but 263. Further regimental establishments are noted in the text to the colour plates.

For comparison, a typical French regiment (after the company re-organizations completed about 1808) consisted of four battalions, each comprising six companies of 140 all ranks each, the regiment (including staff, etc.) therefore consisting of about 3,400 men. A typical 'actual strength' of a well-constituted regiment is provided by a return of the 14th Line: 134 officers, 378 N.C.O.s, 13 pioneers, 54 musicians, 167 grenadiers, 241 voltigeurs and 2,307 fusiliers.

Whereas the French commonly sent drafts of recruits to make extant units up to strength, the British tended to allow battalions to dwindle until sometimes too weak to take the field; on occasion 'provisional battalions' were formed by the amalgamation into one unit of two weak battalions (see Plate 16). A further Peninsula innovation were the British 'battalions of detachments', recovered invalids or detached platoons formed into cohesive units for service in the field or until they could re-join their original corps. For example, the 2nd Battn of detachments which fought at Talavera had one company from the 92nd Highlanders and others from the 42nd, 79th and 95th Rifles.

The French adopted this practice to a greater extent, forming 'provisional' corps of cavalry and infantry to create extra units out of stragglers or to provide escorts without seriously weakening any one unit; Parquin describes one such escort composed of an officer and twenty-five men from each of eight regiments. The 13th Cuirassiers, for example, was organized from the 1st Provisional Heavy Cavalry, initially composed of men from the 1st, 2nd and 3rd Cuirassiers and 1st and 2nd Carabiniers.

Spain

The Spanish regular army emerged from the Peninsular War with an abysmal reputation. Years of corrupt administration had created a hopeless situation of (in Leith Hay's words) 'a Spanish army – ill-commanded, ill-appointed, moderately disciplined and in most respects inefficient ...' Unit sizes were archaic, infantry companies of 188-man establishment with only three officers, clumsy even if trained – which most were not. Voluntary enlistment was assisted by a conscription which took in only the lowest classes. The worst deficiency was the lack of a reliable officer-corps, described by Surtees of the British 95th as 'the most contemptible creatures that I ever beheld ... utterly unfit and unable to command their men'. Promotion (and incentive) was stagnant; those officers (officially one-third) drawn from the ranks had virtually no chance of rising beyond captain; the remainder were aristocrats and landowners (a cavalry commission depended upon having proof of noble blood), many both incapable and disinterested. There was virtually no officer-training, and not even an official drill, so that each colonel instructed his men in his own fashion.

Godoy's progressive weakening of the army created utter chaos. Units were hopelessly under-strength and some cavalry units so short of horses that not one man in three could be mounted. No troops on earth could have decent morale under such conditions, still less if half-equipped and starving. The best of the Spanish army had been 'loaned' to Napoleon for service in northern Europe under the Marqués de la Romana; comprising the cavalry regiments Rey, Infante and Algarbe, the Almansa and Villaviciosa Dragoons, 1st Barcelona and 2nd Catalonian Light Infantry and line regiments Asturias, Princesa, Guadalahara and Zamora, they rebelled on receipt of the news from Spain, successfully rendezvoused with a British squadron and were shipped home, where they formed a reliable nucleus; but even they, in the words of 'TS' of the British 71st, 'had more the appearance of a large body of peasants ... in want of everything, than a regular army'. On the Corunna campaign Surtees commented: 'worse, if possible, in point of appearance than ourselves; but they, in their best days, are more like an armed mob than regularly organized soldiers'.

The commanders were worse than their troops. Excluding exceptions like La Romana and the many officers of foreign descent (principally Irish) they were unreliable, deceiptful and incapable. They supplied Moore with wrong information causing the Corunna débâcle, they left Wellington unsupported and unsupplied after Talavera. Until Wellington assumed personal command of the Spanish troops, that part of the allied army was totally unreliable.

Never under British control to the same extent as the Portuguese, the Spanish remained undistinguished, the cavalry being so useless that their good performances were regarded with amazement. The infantry was panicky, William Warre of the Portuguese Staff describing how regiments ran away (1809): 'The loss I most regret on these occasions are the arms, which the fools throw away in their flight ...' The British, treated with reserve and unco-operation by the Spanish people, and remembering disgraceful episodes like the arrogance and deceipt of Cuesta, maintained a low regard of the Spaniards even when they behaved bravely; Green of the 95th calls them 'bad-plucked ones; they would rather run than fight!' To be fair, the Spanish regulars (such as Morillo's Division in the Pyrenees) fought well when commanded by good officers and receiving (in Wellington's words) 'regular pay and food, and good care and clothing'. Late in the war a limited number of Spaniards were admitted to British regiments, those in the 95th for example behaving admirably.

The civilian combatants and guerrillas were different. Fired by vehement patriotism and supported by the church and most landowners, the defenders of such as Saragossa and Gerona accomplished incredible feats of endurance and bravery – and displaying the greatest cruelty, prompting French retaliation and turning the war into a hideous vendetta.

The Bonapartist forces – the army of King Joseph – was even more wretched than the Spanish regulars. His Royal-Étranger Regt (Royal Foreigners) was raised at Napoleon's suggestion, 'to clear off the crowd of strangers who swarm in Madrid'; the other regiments, according to Napoleon, were of use only 'as a refuge for numbers of people who would otherwise become bandits', and should never be allowed nearer than ten leagues to Madrid as they were so untrustworthy! Many recruits were ex-prisoners of war who deserted at the first opportunity. The Guard units originally recruited from French conscripts were of higher quality.

Portugal

Prior to Beresford's re-organization the Portuguese army was in much the same state as the Spanish, the bulk disbanded by Junot and re-assembled as best it could. Officers were ill-paid and offered no incentives; the British colonel of the 14th Portuguese Line (Le Mesurier) commented that two-thirds of his officers in 'opinions, manners and appearance' were lower than British sergeants and no better educated. Promotion was so limited that the 14th's senior captain had 37 years service and the senior ensign 16; the three senior cornets of one cavalry regiment totalled 180 years of age, whilst the 4th Line had one major who was useless in the field due to lack of experience and 'unwieldy bulk' and a second major a prisoner of the Inquisition!

William Warre, an English officer transferred to the Portuguese staff, gives an unbiased view of the army, being born in Portugal and considering the inhabitants his countrymen. In 1808 he remarked on the 'Portuguese cowards, who won't fight a 1/16th of a Frenchman with arms, but plunder and murder the wounded ...' By 1809 he reported 'The men, poor fellows, are well enough, very obedient, willing, and patient, but also naturally dirty and careless of their persons ... The Officers ... are detestable, mean, ignorant ... little mean intrigues ... apathy ... want of military sentiment ...'

Beresford arranged that from company level upwards British officers were mixed in, only about 200 in the army at any one time (of the 350 combatants and ten doctors who served between 1809 and 1814, 45 were killed in action, thirteen died and two were cashiered for misconduct). Portuguese officers with 'long habits of disregard of duty' were retired, and conscription remedied the lack of strength (Beresford found the army 30,000 strong instead of the establishment of almost 60,000). British officers were placed so that any Portuguese of field rank or higher had British above and below him, and vice-versa; a Portuguese brigade-commander would have two British colonels under his command, whilst a regiment with a British major would have a Portuguese colonel and senior captain, and so on. With capable officers came N.C.O.s and men with better pay, discipline, food and clothing – and therefore higher morale.

Despite rapid improvements, some deficiencies in the Portuguese army were never remedied – unreliable cavalry with insufficient horses and an antiquated siege train, for example. As early as April 1809 Warre wrote that 'The Portuguese immediately under the instruction of British officers are coming on very well ... The men may be made anything we please of, with proper management ...'; by December 1809, 'had they justice done unto them in the common comforts ... clothing and food, they would make as good soldiers as any in the world. None are certainly more intelligent or willing, or bear hardships and privation more humbly', though the officers he found still riddled with 'imbecility and mean contemptible jealousy and intrigue ... though now there are really many very promising young Officers ...' A 'Private Soldier' of the British 27th, writing of Badajos in 1811, notes an officer of the Elvas Regt who 'commenced a precipitate retreat' when the French began to fire, his sergeant rallying the privates who behaved with 'utmost bravery' despite being conscripts, which levies the 'Private Soldier' described joining their regiments roped together and escorted by cavalry, 'dirty and ragged ... barefooted and covered with large broad-brimmed hats', but when uniformed became 'athletic young fellows'.

In spite of the odd prejudiced Englishman (Rifleman Costello considered them 'the noisiest and dirtiest brutes I ever came across. I never knew them to perform one act of gallantry'), by 1812 the Portuguese army had won a fine reputation. In April 1812 Warre stated that although their natural laziness caused them to work only half as hard as the British, 'It is difficult to say which troops, the British or Portuguese, are the most indifferent to danger'. General Picton (a harsh judge) considered the Portuguese and British 'equal in their exertion and deserving an equal portion of laurel'; Judge-Advocate Larpent remarked in 1813 that they looked 'at least equal to ours and better than some'; and Wellington termed them 'the fighting cocks of the army' whose merits owed 'more to the care we have taken of their pockets and bellies than to the instruction we have given them'.

The Portuguese camp-followers and mule-drivers were totally different; they were responsible not only for most of the pillaging blamed on the army but also for the wholesale murder of wounded Frenchmen and much of the corpse-robbing after every battle. The Spanish camp-followers were even worse, one burgling the Commissary-General in 1814 and making off with £2,000 in gold! Ross-Lewin of the British 32nd tells a horrific story of one unscrupulous camp-follower selling 'pork slices' to hungry British troops – cut off a dead Frenchman!

The French Allies

French forces in the Peninsula included a large number of 'foreign' troops, some integral parts of the French army and others from allied states and the French-dominated Confederation of the Rhine. As early as May 1810 William Warre wrote of the disinterested German and Italian conscripts, 'remarkably fine men, and very well clothed, but they complain of never being paid, and that the French treat them like "canaille". Nor have they enough to eat. Many more would desert, but they are afraid of the Spanish and Portuguese peasantry, who murder every thing that wears a French uniform. Yesterday 23 went through ... Prussians taken at Jena and forced to serve. They told me they had rather serve us than the enemies of their country. I never saw finer men.' With desertion *en masse* in 1813 the remaining Confederation troops were disarmed and interned by the French.

Other 'French' contingents included Poles and Swiss of fine quality, reliable Italians and abysmal Neapolitans; details of these and other nationalities serving on both sides can be found in the text to individual plates. Many 'French' regiments were composed of assorted foreigners from all spheres of French influence, many serving unwillingly; Surtees of the British 95th mentions a private of the French 2nd Light Infantry who surrendered most amicably on account of being only a 'pauvre Italien'!

UNIFORMS OF THE PENINSULAR WAR

Whilst most regulation patterns, and many unofficial variations, are described in the text to the colour plates, some preliminary notes are necessary. Many of these concern the British army, not entirely due to the large numbers of participants whose memoirs record the minutia of their uniforms and equipment in closer detail than those of other nationalities appear to have done, but equally by concentrating on one army a more comprehensive picture of how every army was affected can be drawn.

Initially should be noted the slight fallacy of describing anything as, for example, '1812-pattern'; though official patterns were established many uniforms were made by tailors with only written descriptions to refer to, or replaced on campaign by garments of whatever material was available; thus both sides wore many brown uniforms, utilizing the local cloth of the Iberian Peninsula. Idiosyncracies of individuals or regimental colonels resulted in different patterns worn by the officer or in some cases the entire regiment. These differences in 'regulation' versions partly explain the number of contemporary authorities at variance; thus it is difficult to say *exactly* what was worn by a particular regiment at a certain date.

The many written memoirs by Peninsular veterans give an enormous number of examples of such non-regulation costume, providing they were accurately recorded. Whilst the memory may be fallible in recording a battle, a soldier can usually recollect what he was wearing, particularly if his uniform were modified in an unusual manner. Variations on regulation dress, often officially instituted, are more difficult to detect. A few examples are given below, being points not covered in the text to the plates.

The use of ornate 'full dress' was restricted, but quite often was seen in action. Parquin of the French 20th Chasseurs à Cheval records his major's appearance on a day of battle: beard trimmed, moustache waxed, clean shirt and gauntlets, busby with plume and full-dress horse-furniture covered with cowrie shells. Parquin commented on this immaculate turn-out, the Major replying: 'This is how one should look when one is meeting the enemy; one is never too well dressed when the cannon roars.' This attitude was not restricted to officers, Surtees of the British 95th noting at Barrossa a French regiment whose grenadiers and voltigeurs had large plumes on their shakos, red and yellow-over-green respectively, a decoration normally reserved for parade. Its use in action was so limited, however, that Surtees remarked on it presumably, the only occasion he saw it.

Variations on regulation uniform included such practices as wearing shakos back-to-front and marching with arms reversed in moonlight (as did the British 2nd Division near Sare in November 1813, for example), to prevent a tell-tale glint from shako-plate or musket, and the common habit of being officially allowed to wear the jacket-collar unfastened with stock removed in hot weather or when going into action (as at Badajos where the storming-parties also wore trousers rolled up to or above the knees).

A uniform unique to the British army was that of 'volunteer'; young men unable to purchase a commission were allowed to join a regiment in the hopes of being granted a commission after some heroic incident. They wore officers' uniform minus epaulettes but with gold or silver lace shoulder-straps, carried a musket and had privates' cross-belts. Lieut. Simmons of the 95th described a uniform for his brother, about to join the 34th as a volunteer: if a regimental jacket were too expensive, it was quite in order to buy any red coat with white facings, a second-hand sash and sword, a 'common rough' greatcoat, 'any colour, it is of no consequence', and enough pasteboard, oil-silk, black ribbon and 'broad stuff for a binding' for the regimental tailor to make into a cheap imitation of a cocked hat! Two tailors' orders sent from the Peninsula show how flexible 'regulation' dress could be: General Long ordered two sword-belts, 'embroidered or stitched with gold' (no design specified), whilst Capt. Dyneley of the Royal Horse Artillery ordered from Hawkes the cap-maker a forage-cap 'much such another as Lieutenant Macdonald of Ross's troop had of him a short time since. If Hawkes does not recollect, send me one "neat but not gaudy".'

Most armies dressed their musicians in a more colourful uniform than the rest. In the British army the practice of 'reversed colours' was common, the body of the garment made of the regimental facing-colour. This was officially prohibited from September 1811 in consequence 'upon their loss in action, which is ascribed to the marked difference of their dress', musicians' status to be marked in future only by lace. Despite this order many distinctive uniforms continued in use, the 5th Foot for example having white drummers' coats faced red (Inspection Return,

1813). Even medal-ribbons were seen in incorrect colours, Wellington asking in March 1813 for correct ribbon to be sent to each recipient of the Portuguese Order of the Tower and Sword, as 'I saw one yesterday with the cross hanging on a red riband'.

At the beginning of the war the British army still wore the hair in a powdered 'queue' (pigtail). A General Order of 20 July 1808 abolished it, officers to 'take care that the men's hair is cut close in their necks in the neatest and most uniform manner'. Whilst some units complied immediately (the 28th, at sea, hurling the cut queues overboard with three cheers), others were less prompt; the 29th wore theirs at Rolica, and 'TS' of the 71st (if his memory were accurate) records his queue being frozen to the ground at Salamanca in December 1808.

1812 saw a widespread change of pattern in many armies, the so-called 'Bardin' regulations introduced in France and the adoption of 'Belgic' shako and French-style cavalry uniform by the British. Such changes were often delayed for years, existing clothing being allowed to wear out and units on campaign often being unable to receive or make new uniforms. Possibly the 'Belgic' cap was never worn in the Peninsula except by units arriving after 1813, whilst many French units wore pre-1812 styles as late as 1814. Combinations of two styles (see Plate 5) were probably frequent. The British 1812 cavalry uniforms (though handsome) were almost universally condemned as being too French, but the new infantry uniform was more serviceable though unpopular from a sartorial angle.

Wellington's comments on uniform are vital in assessing their effect on the battlefield and partly explain why such laxity of dress was allowed in his army. Writing in November 1811 he had little good to remark on the anticipated uniform-changes: 'There is no subject of which I understand so little ... I think it indifferent how a soldier is clothed, provided it is in a uniform manner; and that he is forced to keep himself clean and smart, as a soldier ought to be'. He quoted the capture of an 11th Light Dragoons officer to illustrate 'one thing I deprecate ... any imitation of the French, in any manner. It is impossible to form an idea of the inconveniences and injury which result from having anything like them ... Lutyens and his picquet were taken ... because the 3rd Hussars had the same caps as the French Chasseurs à Cheval and some of their hussars; and I was near being taken on the 25th September from the same cause. At a distance, or in action, colors [sic] are nothing; the profile, and shape of a man's cap, and his general appearance, are what guide us; and why should we make our people look like the French? ... there is no such mark as the English helmet, and ... it is the best cover a dragoon can have for his head ... I only beg that we may be as different as possible from the French in everything. The narrow top caps of our infantry, as opposed to their broad top caps, are a great advantage to those who look at long lines of posts opposed to each other.'

To illustrate the way in which uniforms could influence events on the battlefield (apart from numerous occasions when uniforms were wrongly identified) is the case of the British 71st in October 1810, who tricked the French by wearing greatcoats and covering the shako-badge and diced cap-band with an issue of black crepe; imagining them to be mere Portuguese militia, the French advanced incautiously and were bloodily repulsed.

On campaign, uniforms naturally became dirty, eventually ragged and patched and frequently fell to pieces before replacements could be issued, necessitating the use of any garment which could be made, looted or dragged off a corpse. The famous passage by Grattan of the 88th could describe almost any regiment in the war: 'Provided we brought our men into the field well appointed, and with sixty rounds of good ammunition each, he [Wellington] never looked to see whether their trousers were black, blue or grey ... we might be rigged out in all colours of the rainbow if we fancied ... scarcely two officers were dressed alike! Some with braided coats, others with brown; some again liked blue; while many from choice, or perhaps necessity, stuck to the "old red rag".'

Pictorial sources of Peninsular uniforms – 'eye-witness' sketches drawn from life – are more limited. A list of contemporary artists whose work has been consulted can be found in the bibliography, but a few deserve further mention. Of particular value are the drawings of Major T. S. St Clair and Capt. Robert Batty, the artist (perhaps a Spanish monk) known only as 'El Guil', and the anonymous artist of the sketches known as 'The Frankfurt Collection' whose work has been valuably recorded by D. S. V. Fosten and R. J. Marrion in issues of *Tradition*. Other artists consulted include Denis Dighton (*some* of whose Peninsular work was apparently drawn from life), Cornelius and Christophe Suhr who recorded uniforms seen in Hamburg (including La Romana's Division), and other well-known contemporary authorities such as C. H. Smith and Martinet. The more modern artists consulted include the exceptionally valuable work of L. Rousselot, E. Leliepvre, 'Rigo' (A. Rigondaud) and 'JOB' (J. Onfroy de Bréville) as well as the Knötel and Bucquoy series.

Many veterans recorded the deterioration of uniforms on campaign. For example, Cooper of the 7th: 'ragged, shirtless, stockingless, and shoeless'; Ross-Lewin of the 32nd (1814): 'No one ... could possibly have discovered ... the original colour of our clothing, for it was so patched with a diversity of colours, and so bespoke a variety of wretchedness that ... we must have borne an undesirable resemblance to Falstaffe's ragged regiment'. In ordeals like the Corunna retreat, uniforms disappeared altogether, Capt. Bogue recalling a terrible figure in 'tatter'd rags of an old black coat' – a member of the 28th. Even so, soldiers continued to be reprimanded for ragged dress, Rifleman Harris noting one Thomas Higgins of the 95th who deserted after being scolded for 'his dress ... almost dropping from his lower limbs, and his knapsack hanging by a strap or two down about his waist.'

First to suffer from campaigning was uniform-dye, the British 'scarlet' (initially a brick-red for other ranks) discolouring until (as with the 40th) 'as ragged as sheep and as black as rooks'. Poor-quality dye ran with rain or sweat, the 50th's black facings at Vimiero originating the nickname 'Dirty Half-Hundred' when the dye was transferred to the men's perspiring faces. Ingrained dust changed colours, Engineer Capt. Landmann recalling how in August 1808 he compared his blue sleeve with Major-General Fane's red, to find hardly any difference in colour.

Patches came in all materials and colours, uniforms (as in the 91st) repaired with grey cloth and some 'with one half of the sleeves a different colour from the body' (Anton). Brown local cloth was most common, though some (like the 29th at Talavera) using white and grey; some uniforms became so patched that 'it was difficult to tell to what regiment we belonged, for each man's coat was like Joseph's "a coat of many colours"' (Wheeler of the 51st). Ultimately whole items – usually trousers – had to be manufactured from local cloth.

Individual costumes adopted of necessity were more bizarre: Lieut. Cadell of the 28th on the Corunna retreat made a poncho from a blanket with a hole cut out, whilst an officer of the 29th on returning from Corunna was mistaken for a captured French general due to his braided pelisse and fancy waistcoat with Spanish filigree buttons! Further examples are noted in the text to individual plates. In desperate circumstances units were *ordered* to discard their kit, the 95th in the Corunna campaign, for example, being told to retain only a greatcoat or blanket; Rifleman Green noted the result of throwing away razors produced 'beards like Jews'. Throughout the war, the 95th veterans were usually so tanned and bearded as to be frequently mistaken for Portuguese. This unit, incidentally, celebrated St Patrick's Day by wearing sprigs of 'leaves, grass or boughs of trees' on their uniform (Costello).

Captured items were widely used, for example the 20th's French trousers in the Pyrenees, Highlanders wearing white French greatcoats after Vimiero, the 18th Hussars parading in December 1808 with captured dragoon buff belts and gauntlets, and the 28th's grenadiers using French hide knapsacks captured in Egypt until at least 1815. Examples are endless, the most surprising being the *purchase* of trousers by British officers in the Pyrenees – from the French opposing them! On occasion British troops wore Spanish cockades to demonstrate 'solidarity', Moore issuing an order in October 1808 that 'in compliment to the Spanish nation, the Army will wear the Red Cockade in addition to their own'. Private Gunn of the 42nd records these as 'scarlet cloth about the size of a hal'penny to wear in front of our bonnets', which were all thrown away within a day!

In less well-supplied armies – Spanish and French – deterioration of uniforms was even more marked. Widely-used by the French were shako-covers, usually white or unbleached, 'white caps' becoming a nickname with the British. The French habit of wearing moustaches was often remarked upon by their opponents, 'TS' of the 71st for example noting French 'beards, long and black', making them appear like 'savages', and Harris the 'tremendous-looking moustaches' of the grenadiers of the 70th Line.

As early as November 1808 Napoleon wrote 'how shamefully I am treated; I have only 1,400 coats, 7,000 great-coats instead of 50,000, 15,000 pairs of shoes instead of 129,000. I am in want of everything; nothing can be worse than clothing. My army will begin the campaign naked; it has nothing. The conscripts are not clothed...' The immediate remedy was to establish clothing factories near to the army, producing hastily-made uniforms probably not including the intricate details of regulation dress; brown Spanish cloth was widely used (see Plate 45). British uniforms were in great demand by invalids and stragglers, Sgt Nicol describing how terrified Frenchmen would wear red coats (and even kilts), hoping thus to avoid being murdered by the Spanish!

Lieut. Francois of the 5th Légion de Réserve describes a typical 'campaign' uniform worn by himself in 1810: a shabby greatcoat belonging to the bandmaster of the 16th Light Infantry, cotton trousers and shoes from an officer of the same, and a grey cloth cap. He had been a prisoner for some time but such 'uniforms' were not uncommon in the field.

The above are random examples taken from contemporary writings which illustrate how non-uniform a 'uniform' could become; many more are described and illustrated in the Colour Plates. A final comment on uniforms of the Peninsular War is provided by Ensign Frederick Mainwaring of the British 51st:

'No one thought about the cut of a coat, or the fashion of a boot, or looked coldly on his neighbour because his ragged garment was less fashionable than his own; sufficient was it that he had a coat on his back.'

EQUIPMENT AND CAMPAIGN KIT

Though equipment is covered in the text to the plates, it is of interest to record the following typical British infantry regulation equipment as described by Sgt Cooper of the 7th (weight in pounds in parentheses): musket and bayonet (14), pouch containing 60 rounds of ball ammunition (6), canteen and belt (1), mess-tin (1), knapsack and belts (3), white undress jacket ($\frac{1}{2}$), two shirts and three 'breasts' ($2\frac{1}{2}$), two pairs shoes (3), trousers (2), gaiters ($\frac{1}{4}$), two pairs stockings (1), four brushes, button-stick and comb (3), cross-belts (1), pen, ink and paper ($\frac{1}{4}$), pipe-clay (1), two tent pegs ($\frac{1}{2}$), three days' bread (3), two days' beef (2) and water in canteen (3). 'Issue' equipment might also include haversack, extra ammunition, camp-kettle and billhook shared by five men (the latter a cumbersome tool, often 'exchanged' for a lighter and better-tempered Portuguese civilian type), plus greatcoat or blanket weighing between four and six pounds. The use of blanket and greatcoat together was rare, an article by 'Militaris' in the *United Services Journal* (1831) claiming that a 'soldier's blanket and greatcoat are more than he can carry. The Duke of Wellington tried it in the year that his army entered France, but it distressed the troops greatly.' Men styled 'handicrafts' (i.e. cobbler, tailor, etc.) also carried the tools of their trade, plus any personal impedimenta picked up *en route*

The constricting belts and heavy load caused exhaustion and even death. Costello of the 95th described his equipment: knapsack and straps, two shirts, two pairs stockings, one pair shoes, one pair spare soles and heels, three brushes, blacking-box, razor, soap-box, spare trousers, mess-tin, ball-bag containing thirty rounds, haversack, canteen, belt and pouch containing fifty rounds of ball ammunition, mallet to hammer balls down the rifle, sword-belt, sword and rifle, plus four bill-hooks per squad. He claimed this 70–80 pound weight caused the death of 400 of his regiment until experienced troops discarded such items as shirts and spare shoes to lighten the load. In 1813 the Light Division received a linen bag to strap on to the knapsack to hold three days' supply of biscuit; these were withdrawn when the men persisted in eating the whole lot on the first day!

Most officers owned much larger kit than their men, being allowed horses or mules as transport (in 1809 Wellington rescinded the order that officers should carry knapsacks, in order to increase mobility and lessen fatigue). The number of officers' baggage-animals was considerable, due to the number allowed senior officers: subalterns (one), majors (seven), lieutenant-colonels commanding battalions (ten), etc. (General Order, 1 September 1809). Even this allowance was often exceeded and included swarms of rascally Spanish and Portuguese muleteers. This accumulation of private baggage (in addition to ordinary supply-trains and regimental baggage-carts) prompted the French General Foy (accustomed to French armies living off the land) to compare the 'mass of impedimenta and camp-followers trailing behind the British' with 'the army of Darius. Only when you had met them in the field do you realise that you have to do with the soldiers of Alexander.'

Typical officers' kit (belonging to Capt. Ferguson of the 2/95th, mortally wounded at Salamanca) included: one tarpaulin bed, pair saddle-bags, set of handkerchiefs, portmanteau, two pairs gloves, pair braces, pair spurs, morning gown, writing-case, six towels, silver watch, two pairs trousers, saddle and bridle, three pairs boots, eight silk handkerchiefs, belt, canteen, waistcoat, spy-glass, six shirts, flannel drawers, sash, looking-glass, eleven pairs socks, dressing brushes, shaving case.

George Simmons of the 95th listed the items required by his brother Joseph, Volunteer in the 34th (1811): dark fustian haversack, uniform jacket, white kerseymere waistcoat, two pairs of grey trousers 'made wide like sailors' trousers', three pairs shoes, 'strong leather gaiters', three pairs socks, second-hand sash and 'cheap' sword; clasp-knife, fork, spoon, tin mug, two or three tooth-brushes and three towels.

Officers in the forefront of the war had little chance to carry canteens of cutlery, lace tablecloths and patent beds. Kincaid of the 95th described his personal kit: 'A haversack on service is a sort of dumb waiter ... a well regulated one ought never to be without the following furniture ... a couple of biscuits, a sausage, a little tea and sugar, a knife, fork and spoon, a tin cup (which answers to the names of tea-cup, soup-plate, wine-glass and tumbler), a pair of socks, a piece of soap, a tooth-brush, towel, and comb, and a half a dozen cigars'. Both Kincaid and Simmons record the use of rudimentary sleeping-bags made from two blankets stitched down the sides.

SHOES

Footwear was a major pre-occupation of the Peninsular armies. The Spanish and Portuguese, used to wearing light sandals, were better off than the French and British, for whom the problem was desperate; for example, in May 1809 Wellington reported his forces lacking 20,000 pairs!

The British 'military shoe' (a term which puzzled even the author of the 'Regimental Companion', an 1804 manual) was frequently of wretched quality; Rifleman Green records his pair having the soles simply glued on by an unscrupulous contractor, thus falling to pieces rapidly. Hard campaigning reduced the army to a barefoot state which not even widespread corpse-robbing could remedy, and even prompted Green into verse: 'Blister'd feet, worn out stockings, and boots without soles/Are the portion of many, who go out to war'. The fact that British troops had to buy new shoes themselves (extra to the two pairs issued per year) added insult to injury!

On the Corunna retreat the shoe situation became chronic; 'TS' of the 71st notes that even 'officers of the Guards, and others, worth thousands', trudged along with feet wrapped in torn blankets, some malicious individuals pointing at them and remarking: 'There goes three thousand a year!' Officers were usually in the same plight as their men, Green recording them offering a guinea a pair for common shoes, while Rifleman Harris particularly remembered Lieut. Hill of the 95th as being 'one of the few amongst us in the possession of a tolerably decent pair of boots'; at the end of the campaign the entire regiment was 'in a ghastly state ... feet swathed in bloody rags ...'

Almost every Peninsula reminiscence mentions the problem; Cooper of the 7th states that it was usual for a hundred of his regiment to be shoeless at any one time. The remedy varied: Surgeon Brookes of the 87th resorted to house-breaking in 1809 to avoid the fate of the rest of his regiment, totally incapacitated by cut feet after marching over sharp rocks. Capt. Verner of the 7th Hussars, *en route* to Corunna, wore 'brown Spanish leather shoes', only obtained by standing over an unwilling shoemaker until they were finished; as soon as any man fell by the wayside, wrote Verner, dead or not, 'his boots were on another person's legs'.

Spanish sandals were extensively used, easily-manufactured from raw bullock-hide, and so popular that Lt-Col. Stepney records the unwillingness of his Guards in 1812 to use captured French boots in place of their comfortable sandals. In the following year they were issued with light hemp sandals, better-suited for climbing the Pyrenees than the regulation boots.

Regimentally-manufactured boots varied in style; Cadell of the 28th records how in 1812 a stray bullock was seized and cut up with as much relish for hide as for meat, being made into sandals by the regimental cobblers. Highlanders made 'cuarans' or Highland moccasins from hide – horse-hide for the 42nd on the Corunna retreat, for example, though even so the members of this unit were allowed to break ranks and walk on softer earth with their bare feet. Other more bizarre types of footwear included the wooden shoes as a protection against deep mud, recorded by Lieut. Hay of the 12th Light Dragoons.

Britain

1 a) General Officer of Hussars, 1813.
b) Lieut. Gen. Sir John Moore, 1808.

Britain

2 a) Officer, 1st Dragoons, 1809.
  b) Officer, 4th Dragoons, 1811.

Britain

3 a) – top – Officer, 2nd Life Guards, 1813.
  b) – below – Trooper, 3rd Dragoons, 1812.

Britain

4 a) Officer, 16th Light Dragoons, 1810.
  b) Trooper, 15th Light Dragoons (Hussars), 1809.

Britain

5 a) Trooper, 9th Light Dragoons, 1813.
b) Officer, 12th Light Dragoons, 1812-13.

Britain

6 a) Officer, Battalion Company, with Regimental Colour, 4th Foot, 1808.
b) Officer, Light Company, 4th Foot, 1808.

Britain

7 a) Sergeant, Battalion Company, 31st Foot, 1809.
  b) Private, 23rd Fusiliers, 1809.
  c) Private, Battalion Company, 5th Foot, 1809.

Britain

8 a) Officer, Light Company, 45th Foot, 1812.
b) Infantry officer in greatcoat, 1810.

Britain

9 a) Colour-Sergeant, Grenadier Company, 87th Foot, 1814.
b) Corporal, Battalion Company, 1st Foot Guards, undress, 1814.

Britain

10 a) Piper, 71st (Highland) Light Infantry, 1812.
   b) Private, Grenadier Company, 92nd Highlanders, 1814.

11 a) Officer, 52nd Light Infantry, 1813.
b) Officer, 43rd Light Infantry, 1812.

Britain

12 a) Officer, 95th Rifles, campaign uniform, 1810-12.
    b) Bugler, 95th Rifles, 1808.
    c) Officer, 95th Rifles, 1811.

Britain

13 a) Private, 5th Battn, 60th (Royal American) Regt, 1812.
b) Officer, 5th Battn, 60th (Royal American) Regt, 1814.

Britain

14 a) Corporal, Royal Artillery, 1808.
b) Quartermaster, Royal Horse Artillery, 1814.

15 a) Private, Royal Sappers and Miners, 1814.
   b) Officer, Royal Engineers, 1814.

Britain

16 a) Officer with Colour, Provisional Battn de Roll-Dillon.
b) Officer, Light Company, Chasseurs Britanniques, 1812.

Britain

17 a) Officer, 2nd Dragoons, King's German Legion, campaign dress, 1810.
   b) Officer, 2nd Dragoons, King's German Legion, drill order, 1810.

Britain

18 a) Officer, Battalion Company, 1st Line Battn, King's German Legion, 1811.
   b) Assistant-Surgeon, 5th Line Battalion, King's German Legion, 1813.

Britain

19 a) Private, Loyal Lusitanian Legion, 1809.
   b) Jäger, Brunswick Oels Corps, 1812.
   c) Private, Rifle Company, Calabrian Free Corps, 1812.

Portugal

20 a) Staff Officer, 1811.
   b) General.

Portugal

21 a) Trooper, 3rd Cavalry, 1809.
   b) Officer, 10th Cavalry, 1812.

Portugal

22 a) Sergeant, 18th Infantry.
   b) Officer, 21st Infantry, with Colour.

23 a) Private, 20th Infantry.
   b) Corporal, Light Company, 4th Infantry, 1811.
   c) Private, Algarve Volunteers.

Portugal

24 a) Officer, 18th Militia.
b) Private, 18th Militia.
c) Private, Militia.

Portugal

25 a) Private, 4th Caçadores, 1812.
b) Private, 1st Caçadores, 1809.

Portugal

26 a) Gunner, 3rd Foot Artillery, 1808.
    b) Gunner, 2nd Foot Artillery, 1812.
    c) Officer, 5th Caçadores, 1812.

Spain

27 Aides-de-Camp, 1813.

Spain

28 a) Officer, Life Guards, 1808.
   b) Officer, Regt de la Reyna, 1808.
   c) Trooper, Voluntarios de España, 1808.

Spain

29 a) Trooper, Villaviciosa Dragoons, 1808.
b) Officer, Maria Luisa Hussars, 1808.
c) Officer, Numancia Dragoons, 1808.

Spain

30 a) Officer, Regt El Rey, 1808.
b) Trooper, Regt Algarbe, undress, 1807.

Spain

31 a) Drum-Major, Regt Princesa, 1808.
   b) Musician, Regt Princesa, 1808.
   c) Officer, Regt Irlanda, 1808.

Spain

32 a) Grenadier, Regt Zamora, 1808.
    b) Fusilier, Regt de Aragon, 1808.
    c) Pioneer, Regt Princesa, 1808.

Spain

33 a) Officer, 2nd Catalonian Light Infantry, 1808.
   b) Private, 2nd Catalonian Light Infantry, 1808.
   c) Sergeant, Cazadores, Light Infantry, 1813.

Spain

34 a) Officer, Artillery, 1808.
   b) Private, Regt Muerte, 1808.

Spain

35 a) Fusilier Officer, Infantry, 1812.
b) Grenadier, Infantry, 1812.

Spain

36 a) Private, Infantry, 1812.
   b) Cazadore Officer, Infantry, 1812.
   c) Officer, Infantry, 1812.

37 a) Private, Medina Sidonia Regt, 1813.
   b) Officer, Cortes Regt, 1813.

Spain

38 a) Private, Walloon Guards, 1813.
b) Field Officer, Toledo Regt, 1813.

Spain

39 a) Guerrilla officer, 1813.
   b) Guerrilla.
   c) Catalonian volunteer.

France

40 a) Aide-de-Camp, 1813.
b) General Lefebvre-Desnoëttes, 1808.

France

41 a) Private, Young Guard, 1810.
   b) Private, Chasseurs à Pied, Imperial Guard, 1808.
   c) Trumpeter, Marines of the Guard, 1808.

France

42 a) Trooper, 3rd Dragoons, 1810.
b) Officer, 20th Dragoons, 1810.

France

43 a) Officer, 27th Chasseurs à Cheval, 1809.
b) Trooper, 10th Chasseurs à Cheval, 1810.

France

44 a) Trooper, Elite Company, 4th Hussars, 1808.
   b) Officer, 2nd Hussars, 1811.

45 a) Trooper, 13th Cuirassiers, 1810.
b) Maréchal-des-Logis, 1st Lancers, Vistula Legion.

France

46 a) Fusilier, Infantry, 1813.
   b) Grenadier, Infantry, 1809.
   c) Grenadier, 14th Line, 1808.

France

47 a) Voltigeur officer, Infantry, 1812.
   b) Grenadier officer, Infantry, 1809.
   c) Voltigeur hornist, Infantry, 1812.

France

48 a) Drum-Major, 2nd Légion de Réserve.
b) Drum-Major, 15th Line.
c) Drum-Major, 16th Light Infantry, 1812.

France

49 a) Officer, 27th Light Infantry, 1809.
   b) Drummer, 27th Light Infantry, 1809.

France

50 a) Voltigeur, 16th Light Infantry, 1812.
   b) Drum-Major, 17th Light Infantry, 1809.

France

51 Officers, Chasseurs de Montagne.

France

52 a) Voltigeur, 2nd Paris Municipal Guard, 1808.
   b) Fusilier officer, 2nd Paris Municipal Guard, 1809.
   c) Grenadier, 1st Paris Municipal Guard, 1808.

France

53 a) Trooper, Lanciers-Gendarmes, Gendarmerie d'Espagne, 1811.
b) Trooper, Gendarmes à Cheval, Gendarmerie d'Espagne, 1811.

France

54 a) Sergeant-Major, Régiment de Westphalie, 1808.
b) Officer, Régiment de Prusse, 1808.

55 a) Pioneer, 3rd Swiss Regt, 1808.
b) Chef de Bataillon, Bataillon Valaison, 1808.
c) Voltigeur, Régiment Irlandaise, 1808.

Spain/Berg

56 a) Grenadier, Royal Guard, 1812.
b) Officer, Gardes du Corps Squadron, Chevau-Légers, 1808.

Kingdom of Naples

57 a) Officer, 2nd Chasseurs à Cheval, 1813.
   b) Trumpeter, 1st Chasseurs à Cheval, 1811.

Kingdom of Naples

58 a) Fusilier captain, 8th Line, 1812.
   b) Fusilier, 1st Line, 1808.
   c) Carabinier, 1st Light Infantry, 1811.

Kingdom of Italy

59 a) Officer, Elite Company, 2nd Dragoons, 1811.
   b) Fusilier, 5th Line, 1809.

Westphalia/Saxe-Altenburg

60 a) Grenadier, 3rd Infantry, 1809.
   b) Officer, Infantry, 1808.

Duchy of Warsaw/Nassau/Confederation of the Rhine

61 a) Grenadier N.C.O., 7th Regt, 1810.
   b) Carabinier officer, 2nd Regt, 1813.
   c) Fusilier, Schwarzburg-Sonderhausen Company, 6th Confederation Regt, campaign dress, 1810.

Coburg-Saalfeld/Lippe

62 a) Private, Battn Coburg-Saalfeld, 1809.
   b) Officer, Battn Coburg-Saalfeld, 1809.
   c) Private, Infantry, 1809.

Hesse-Darmstadt

63 a) Officer, Regt Graf und Erbprinz, 1810.
    b) Gunner, Artillery, 1809.
    c) Driver, Artillery Train, 1809.

Cleve-Berg/Baden

64 a) Grenadier, Infantry, 1811.
b) Gunner, Artillery, 1812.

1 **BRITAIN:**
   a) General Officer of Hussars, 1813.
   b) Lieut.-Gen. Sir John Moore, 1808.

Sir John Moore, whose influence on the Peninsular War has been much under-rated, wears the 'unlaced' undress coat frequently worn on campaign and shown in Lawrence's portrait of Moore. The full-dress version had loops of gold 'twist' lace instead of embroidered button-holes. Buttons were evenly-spaced for generals, in pairs for major-generals, and in threes for lieut.-generals. Each uniform had numerous variations; for example, the lapels could be buttoned back to expose a dark blue 'plastron' front. The gold-embroidered epaulettes were replaced in 1811 by a gold aiguillette on the right shoulder. Junior staff officers wore similar uniform, with different lace and frequently blue collars instead of the scarlet with blue collar-patch illustrated. Adjutant- and Quartermaster-Generals wore lieut.-generals' dress with silver lace; their Assistants wore A.D.C. uniform with silver lace and two epaulettes. Majors-of-Brigade wore silver-laced staff uniform, with epaulettes on the right shoulder for infantry and left for cavalry, the latter changing to an aiguillette on the right shoulder in 1811, and both adopting epaulettes on the left in 1814. Aides-de-Camp had basically the Major-of-Brigade uniform with gold lace and tassel-ended loops. Many variations included the use by all ranks of half-laced and half-unlaced uniform.

Moore's hat has a waterproof cover, but in full dress had a black cockade, gold loop and white-over-red feather; there were variations, for example Judge-Advocate-General Larpent's black feather (which he removed at Salamanca, being mistaken for a surgeon), and at Vimiero Rifleman Harris records how General Fane stuck in his hat a green feather taken from a dead Frenchman! Moore wears service overalls, but white breeches and 'Hessian' boots were common, even on campaign. The breast-star is that of the Order of the Bath. Swords were a matter of personal taste, that shown being used by Moore at Corunna.

The General Officer of Hussars' magnificent costume (including leopardskin shabraque and cowrie-shell harness-ornaments) evolved unofficially and probably varied with every wearer. Portraits of Lord Londonderry, Sir Richard Hussey and the Prince Regent, and preserved examples, show a hussar dress with extra-thick braid and cap-lines and sumptuous lacing throughout; Robert Dighton Jnr shows the uniform worn as early as c. 1808, that illustrated primarily taken from a Denis Dighton picture of c. 1814. The shabraque is taken from that of the Marquis of Anglesey, Denis Dighton's version having a crossed-baton device and laurel-branches below the cypher on the rear corners; perhaps the shabraque-design was based on that of the individual's regiment. Lieut. Woodberry of the 18th Hussars proves that this impractical costume was worn in the Peninsular War, describing Sir Stapleton Cotton in July 1813 'dressed in a most superb uniform as General of Hussars – Red and Gold – his staff likewise wore Hussar dresses'.

The regulation staff uniform (its plainness remarked upon by Junot at the Convention of Cintra) was frequently replaced on campaign by civilian garments. Wellington usually wore a small cocked hat, grey or blue frock-coat, white neck-cloth and (as described by Gleig of the 85th) 'grey pantaloons, with boots, buckled at the sides; and a steel-mounted light sabre'. This elegant civilian dress (hence his nickname, 'The Beau') astonished the Spaniards who were used to the glittering cavalcades of their own and French armies. Sir John Colborne records Wellington resembling 'an old White Friar', wearing a short white cloak captured from a French dragoon, while on occasion he wore the sky-blue frock-coat of the Hatfield Hunt. Sir Thomas Picton habitually wore a top-hat to shade his eyes, and a plain coat; at Vittoria, Kincaid records him 'dressed in a blue coat and a round hat, and swore as roundly as if he had been wearing two cocked ones'; Sir G. L'Estrange saw him in the same costume at the Pyrenees, and at Busaco Picton's bizarre dress included a night-cap. His personal staff were so careless in their dress that Picton and Co. were nicknamed 'the bear and ragged staff'!

Greatcoats were often worn on campaign; 'Blue or grey slouch great-coats are worn by all; one may almost say the shabbier the better' (Sir Augustus Frazer); Sir Harry Smith noted General Skerret's 'military blue coat' had pockets large enough to take two bottles of sherry! Regulations specified that Commissaries should wear 'unlaced' scarlet staff uniform with blue collar, cuffs and lapels, button-holes embroidered with 'twist' and two rows of twelve buttons on the breast (the upper one on the collar); and Assistant-Commissaries dark blue single-breasted coats with scarlet collar and cuffs, both with 'One General's epaulet, straps embroidered in blue' (*Regimental Companion*, 1804). Attached non-military personnel wore their own creations, Kincaid recording a Mr Rogers of the Civil Department in 1812 'equipped in a huge cocked-hat, and a hermaphrodite sort of scarlet coat, half military and half civil', while Edward Frith, the 'fighting parson' of the 2nd Division, wore a scarlet dolman.

See also Plate 1, *Uniforms of Waterloo*.

2 BRITAIN:
a) Officer, 1st Dragoons, 1809.
b) Officer, 4th Dragoons, 1811.

Until 1812 British dragoon uniform included large bicorn hat, scarlet coatee with lace loops, and white breeches and long boots in full dress, as worn by the 1st Dragoon illustrated (after Robert Dighton). Officers had chain or scale epaulettes, and other ranks facing-coloured wings and shoulder-straps (dark blue for the 1st and green for the 4th). Lace was white or yellow (silver or gold for officers), the breast-loops tapering towards the waist.

Service dress included a cylindrical undress or 'watering' cap, often with folding peak and regimental badge (the 1st Dragoons, for example, had a motif of '1st D' and a laurel-wreath). Chin-scales were sometimes worn, but the busby-type bag worn earlier in the century had been discontinued. An Inspection Return of the 1st Dragoons in 1804 noted all ranks wearing the cap, as 'they have no hats'; they had hats in the Peninsula, but warped out of shape by the weather: 'no old dustman ... ever wore so filthy or so dusty apology for a hat ...' Lt-Col. Tomkinson of the 16th Light Dragoons wrote in October 1811 that the heavy cavalry had 'got a new set out of Portuguese chapeos (hats)', another officer recording the issue as the first for three years. This uniform lasted at least until spring 1813, when in April Capt. Ralph Heathcote reported the introduction of the 1812 pattern uniform (Plate 3): '... completely changed our appearance ... instead of hats, we now wear helmets very like that of the French Dragoons, a change which altogether is rather better than otherwise ...' Breeches and long boots were usually exchanged on campaign for overalls of varied pattern; in 1811 John Luard of the 4th wrote home for 'moleskin breeches ... to withstand the horrid climate ...' and William Coles for light grey pepper-and-salt cloth to make two pairs of overalls. A Denis Dighton picture of an officer of the 6th Dragoons shows similar overalls with two lace stripes on the seam.

Campaigning soon spoiled the handsome uniform; in 1811 Luard reported that his hair had been bleached by the sun, and that his scarlet jacket was almost the same colour; by March 1814 even the new pattern uniform was faded and patched, helmets battered, and overalls of every colour and cloth. Luard noted one fashion-conscious officer of the 4th who constantly searched for extra lace to ornament his uniform; on his return from foraging his reply to questions about supplies was invariably: 'I don't know, but I found some silver lace.'

3 BRITAIN:
a) Officer, 2nd Life Guards, 1813.
b) Trooper, 3rd Dragoons, 1812.

The 1812 heavy cavalry uniform included a jacket fastened by hooks-and-eyes, with facing-coloured shoulder-straps or twisted shoulder-cords instead of epaulettes; the lace on the breast, collar, cuffs (pointed for dragoons and square-cut for dragoon guards) and turnbacks often had a coloured 'worm' woven in the centre, though plain lace was not unknown. Also introduced in 1812 were a striped girdle and new overalls, the latter usually grey with a coloured stripe but shown by Denis Dighton as light blue with scarlet stripe for the 4th Dragoons.

The new helmet was initially of black leather with brass fittings, side-bars and crest, supporting a woollen 'caterpillar', either dark blue or black with red or crimson cross-bands. A trooper's helmet in the Prince Regent's collection had a felt skull with woollen crest, and an officer's had a beaver skull, silk crest and gilt fittings; both had a crown over reversed 'GR' cypher on the front-plate, white plume, and gilt or brass rose-shaped chinscale-bosses. The helmet, apparently introduced early in 1812, was reported by the War Office to 'appear in every way objectionable' and was replaced, possibly in August 1812, by the familiar version with black horsehair mane (sometimes held in place by a braid or horsehair looped around the rear from the top of the crest), no plume, leather peak, and small oval above the peak bearing the regimental title. There is little conclusive evidence about the date of introduction of either helmet, or whether the striped-crest version was ever worn in the Peninsula.

The Household Cavalry – 1st and 2nd Life Guards and Royal Horse Guards who arrived in the Peninsula in 1813 – wore heavy cavalry uniform and maned helmet. Both Life Guard regiments wore scarlet faced dark blue, and the R.H.G. dark blue faced scarlet, all with gold lace. Overalls varied in colour, Denis Dighton for example showing light blue with gold stripes for the R.H.G. In 1814 sabretaches were adopted, and another new helmet, similar to that illustrated but with a gilt peak for officers and a woollen caterpillar crest of dark blue or black over scarlet. Dighton shows its use by the R.H.G. in 1814 but a Goddard print of the 2nd Life Guards of the same date shows the maned helmet. A print of Vittoria – perhaps unreliable – shows the R.H.G. wearing the heavy cavalry bicorn discontinued in 1812!

The 1812-pattern uniform was unpopular due to the obvious French influence in its design, a writer in the *Royal Military Chronicle* (January 1813) claiming that the heavy cavalry, 'who had one of the handsomest uniforms in any service, are now a sort of modern antique without a similarity, unless, indeed, in the older wardrobes of some of the theatres'. Col. Leach of the 95th, however, noted the Householders' appearance on arrival in the Peninsula as 'fair and beautiful as lillies'.

Facing-colours and lace for other regiments engaged in the Peninsular War were: 3rd Dragoon Guards, white/gold; 4th D.G. dark blue/silver; 5th D.G. green/gold; 1st Dragoons, dark blue/gold. C. H. Smith at this time shows the 4th Dragoons with light blue facings, laced silver. See also Plates 2 and 3, *Uniforms of Waterloo*.

4 BRITAIN:
a) Officer, 16th Light Dragoons, 1810.
b) Trooper, 15th Light Dragoons (Hussars), 1809.

In the 1808-09 campaign the 7th, 10th, 15th and 18th Hussars wore traditional hussar dress – braided dolman, fur-edged pelisse, barrelled sash, either breeches and boots or grey service overalls, and fur busby. The latter was most unpopular, Sir Robert Ker Porter noting that 'flimsy, muff-like appendages encumber the heads of our soldiers. The awkward cap ... constructed partly of pasteboard, soaks up a great quantity of wet ... unbearably heavy and disagreeable ... affords no protection to the wearer ...'; in December 1808 a Dr Neale reported that 'Our Dragoons complain much of their new-fashioned fur caps ... top-heavy, either tumbled off during the charge, or were cut down by the heavy French swords like so much cartridge-paper'. Capt. Gordon of the 15th noted the use of oil-skin cap-covers in the Corunna campaign.

All regiments had dark blue dolmans, with white facings and silver lace for the 7th (blue facings from 1812), yellow with silver for the 10th (scarlet facings from 1811, blue with gold from 1814), scarlet with silver for the 15th and white with silver for the 18th; other ranks' lace yellow or white accordingly. Pelisses were coloured as the dolman, though exceptions included the 7th's band which wore scarlet from 1806. Overalls were of varied pattern; a portrait of Lieut. Brown of the 10th, for example, shows grey overalls with buff leather 'cuffs' and silver seam-stripe piped red on both sides; Dighton shows an N.C.O. of the 10th with the same stripe of white lace; the 15th are shown with a plain red stripe. Plain sabretaches were used on campaign instead of the laced 'dress' version.

On returning to the Peninsula in 1813, the hussars wore a wide-topped shako (except the 18th, which retained the busby with distinctive light blue bag). The 7th's shako is shown by one source as brown beaver fur, though by September 1813 were blue cloth (red for the band); Goddard & Booth and Dighton show the 10th with black peakless caps, though Schaumann records the receipt of scarlet shakos in March 1813. The Adjutant's journal of the 15th records 'fitting of the new caps' on 19 March 1813, 'the wear of Hussar caps discontinued' nine days later. The shako had cap-lines and lace decoration, and often a waterproof cover; see Plates 5 and 6, *Uniforms of Waterloo*.

On 9 March 1813 *The Public Ledger* stated:

'We are glad to find that the tiddy dol appearance of our hussar regiments has, at length, been noticed. That the ingenuity of our army milleners... should be exercised for the purpose of rendering the appearance of our brave fellows ridiculous instead of promoting their health and comfort and security, is much to be lamented... we cannot but think that the fribbling ornaments with which they are attired would better become an equestrian performer on one of our inferior stages, than a hardy veteran, when equipped for the field...'

Horse-furniture varied; Lieut. Woodberry of the 18th noted that the 10th and 15th had their 'Review Furniture' in 1813, though the 18th had only plain service furniture, plus plain blue shabraque for officers' dress occasions; 'we shall not be equal to them in appearance. However... our dress will be more becoming a Regiment on Service...' Regimental Orders of 23 February 1813 stated that the 18th's 'plain bridles and furniture... will have quite as soldierlike appearance as the more splendid Review Furniture of the other two Regiments of Hussars'.

Pelisse-fur was light brown for the 7th (white for officers); officers of the 10th had grey fur and busbies, other ranks white; black fur for the 15th (except N.C.O.s) and grey for the 18th.

Until the introduction of the 1812 uniform, Light Dragoons wore the dark blue braided dolman and fur-crested 'Tarleton' helmet with turban initially of the facing-colour, but by this time often black (shown by R. Dighton for the 16th as early as c. 1801); the plume was frequently omitted on campaign. Facing-colours for Peninsular units were: 9th buff with silver lace (crimson/gold after 1811); 11th pale buff/silver, 12th pale yellow/silver, 13th buff/gold, 14th orange/silver, 16th scarlet/silver, 20th yellow (orange/gold after 1808), 23rd yellow (crimson/silver after 1808). Legwear consisted of breeches and boots (buff breeches for units with buff facings) or overalls; the 1796 light cavalry sabre was carried by all, though many hussar officers favoured 'mameluke-hilted' curved sabres.

Despite objections to the 1812 uniform (Plate 5), some were unenthusiastic about the previous style; Col. Tomkinson of the 16th, for example, disliked the 'Tarleton': 'We... received our new helmets... and not before they were wanted. The old ones were completely worn out, and so warped by the sun that the men could scarcely wear them. They are bad things for a soldier, only looking well for a few months; the first rain puts them out of shape. All the silver to the edging comes off with both men and officers...' Non-regulation forage-caps included that of Lieut. Ker of the 9th in 1813, described by Capt. Bragge: '... a Blue Velvet Foraging Cap, gold tassel and Band of the same edged with white Ermine. How nice'. Chichester and Burges-Short state that the 11th had 'a sort of black velvet képi of regimental pattern'.

5 BRITAIN:
a) Trooper, 9th Light Dragoons, 1813.
b) Officer, 12th Light Dragoons, 1812–13.

The French-style Light Dragoon uniform introduced in 1812 included a 'Polish' jacket with 'plastron' lapels (often buttoned over on campaign to conceal the facing-colour), epaulettes, and bell-topped shako with lace decoration, cockade and rosette, white-over-red plume and black waterproof cover on campaign; officers had cap-lines of mixed crimson-and-gold, and caps in the Prince Regent's collection described as 'Sergeants'' had mixed yellow-and-red cords. Striped girdles – gold and crimson for officers – and sabretaches were other innovations, the latter usually plain black leather on campaign but laced for officers.

Numerous regimental variations existed, the trooper illustrated after C. R. de Berenger, showing an unusually-large plume, and 'dress' breeches and boots. The officer of the 12th wears a 'transitional' uniform, before the 1812 regulations could be fully implemented; from a Heaphy portrait of Col. Ponsonby painted in 1819, it is believed to be based upon a sketch made in the Peninsula. The 1812-pattern jacket (actually authorized in October 1811) is worn with breeches and belts from the previous uniform; the helmet is taken from a Robert Dighton watercolour, with white-over-red plume removed for campaign. The date can be estimated by a letter from John Vandeleur of the 12th, dated 24 December 1812: 'All the new clothing has come out except the caps which we expect every day... We are to wear dark brown overalls with two stripes of yellow down the sides, the officers to wear two stripes of silver'; by 25 January 1813 the regiment wore the new uniform in entirety. The fashion of wearing items of two different patterns was not uncommon; traditionally, at least some officers of the 16th wore the braided dolman at Waterloo. A unique distinction of the 12th was a dark blue pelisse, apparently unbraided, with collar and cuffs of crimson or yellow plush, shown by Dighton and described by Lieut. Thomas Reed, among others. Overalls were usually grey, with facing-coloured stripes and brown leather reinforcing. See Plates 7 and 10, *Uniforms of Waterloo*.

The 1812 uniform provoked intense criticism; Vandeleur wrote that 'our neat little uniform is to be changed to that of a most foreign look', while a vituperative writer in the *Royal Military Chronicle* (1813) claimed that units so dressed would be mistaken for French and set upon by the Spanish: '... absolutely metamorphosed ... to Frenchmen ... at the Horse Guards I observed several nondescripts, and ... was told, to my utter astonishment, that they were Englishmen and soldiers, belonging to the 13th Light Dragoons!!! ... I presume they have been altered and altered till no English alteration remained, and it was therefore necessary to adopt French ones ...' The first appearance of the uniform in January 1812 caused a trooper to be 'hooted and quizzed' by his fellows, with 'Who's that damned Frenchman?' according to Berkeley Paget, who complained that the officers' version would cost £300 and that nothing of the old uniform would 'be convertible to any purpose whatsoever'.

Uniforms naturally deteriorated on campaign; for example, the 9th after the Burgos retreat were 'naked and starving with cold'; Lieut. Bacon of the 16th noted in October 1813 that 'some of the officers have scarce a thread on their backs'; whilst the 13th and 14th were given the nickname 'The Ragged Brigade' in 1813–14, so ragged that the 13th had to patch their overalls with red oilskin taken from baggage-wrappers!

6 BRITAIN:
   a) **Officer, Battalion Company, with Regimental Colour, 4th Foot, 1808.**
   b) **Officer, Light Company, 4th Foot, 1808.**

Prior to the 1812 regulations which introduced short jackets, infantry officers wore long-tailed coats and bicorns. Regiments were distinguished by the colour of the collar, cuffs and (for officers) lapels, and by the spacing and colour of the lace loops; officers of 'unlaced' regiments had embroidered dummy button-holes in place of metallic lace. 'Centre' or 'battalion' companies had white-over-red plumes, epaulettes for officers and tufted shoulder-straps for other ranks; the 'flank' companies (grenadiers and light infantry) had white and green plumes respectively and laced 'wings' (chain or scales for officers).

The 'battalion' officer illustrated wears typical campaign uniform, including rolled blanket, canteen, white breeches and black gaiters (worn by all ranks until the adoption of overall-trousers). Flank companies wore different head-dress, the grenadiers fur caps (not usually taken on active service) and the light companies a 'stovepipe' shako with bugle-horn badge indicative of their rôle; light infantry officers had short jackets like the men. Undress uniform varied, that illustrated being reconstructed from regimental orders: 'Frock coat. Blue cloth, double-breasted, falling collar of scarlet cloth, blue cuffs with slits to open with four small buttons, pockets to open at pleats; sword and sash worn outside'. The officer wears a 'battalion' sash, the corded light infantry pattern not introduced until 1809 according to regimental orders. Swords were of the 1796 pattern, the curved flank company sabre used by many, but personal variations existed. The rectangular gilt shoulder-belt plate had cut corners and bore a silver crowned garter with lion and IV within. Officers of the 4th adopted gold lace in 1809.

The 4th apparently adopted the 'Belgic' shako introduced by the 1812 regulations comparatively quickly, for at San Sebastian (August 1813) Lieut. Maguire led the 'forlorn hope' storming-party wearing a bicorn with white feather, 'to make himself conspicuous and recognisable', which Oman thought indicated that the other officers wore shakos. It proved too conspicuous as Maguire was killed at the breach.

Each battalion had two Colours, a 'King's Colour' consisting of a large Union flag with regimental devices in the centre, and a 'Regimental' Colour, usually of the regimental facing-colour with a small Union in the upper canton nearest the pike, and bearing regimental devices, in this case a crowned Garter with GR in the centre, a small lion in three cantons and the inscription IV OR K.O.RL.RT. on the horizontal arm of the small Union.

7 BRITAIN:
a) Sergeant, Battalion Company, 31st Foot, 1809.
b) Private, 23rd Fusiliers, 1809.
c) Private, Battalion Company, 5th Foot, 1809.

Other ranks' infantry uniform prior to the 1812 regulations included the 'stovepipe' shako with black cockade held by regimental button (often a grenade or bugle-horn for flank companies) and large brass plate, often bearing regimental numbers in addition to the coat-of-arms device; neck-flaps to act as sun-shade were attached to some caps. The jacket bore regimental facings on collar, cuffs and shoulder-straps, and either square-ended or 'bastion'-shaped lace set singly or in pairs (see Appendix I). Woven into the lace was a regimental design; the 31st, for example, had a red line, the 5th two red lines, and the 23rd one red and one blue line. 'Flank' companies and Fusiliers had red wings with white lace and worsted fringe, and 'battalion' companies a white tuft at the end of the shoulder-straps.

The sergeant of the 31st is taken from an eye-witness sketch of (presumably) a prisoner-of-war. The plume identifies a 'battalion' company, but the green cords – not usually worn on the 'stovepipe' – suggest light infantry. The parti-coloured shoulder-tufts are unusual, though an extant jacket of the 26th Foot has similar. Sergeants' rank was indicated by three lace chevrons on a facing-coloured backing, and a crimson waist-sash with central stripe of the facing colour, the man illustrated using his sash to bind up the bottom of his overalls.

The facings of the 5th were 'gosling' green, a yellowish-brown shade. The man wears standard equipment – cross-belts supporting cartridge-box and bayonet, a haversack and knapsack, the latter of 'bag' type, the 'box' pattern being introduced some time before Waterloo. In 1808 all knapsacks were ordered to be painted black, though as late as 1812 'TS' of the 71st notes that his unit's knapsacks were 'black with grease', implying that they were not painted. Regimental badges were often painted on the flap; a Genty picture of 1815 shows the 5th with a crowned Garter with '5' in the centre and 'V' below. The 5th's Inspection Returns note that in 1809 sergeants had plain crimson sashes, in 1810 that the grenadiers' fur caps had not been taken on active service, and in 1813 that officers had black waistbelts instead of shoulder-belts and that the regiment wore feather plumes instead of worsted tufts, perhaps white for all companies, as Sgt Grey's regimental song included the lines:

'Our streaming white feathers are plain to be seen,
And our facings are called the gosling green.'

The fusilier cap was similar to that of the grenadiers, and was probably worn by the 7th and 23rd (at least by N.C.O.s) for a short time at the start of their campaigning, before replaced by the shako. The cap had a cloth rear patch bearing the regimental badge. One line regiment, the 28th, never replaced the 'stovepipe' cap, which had a crown over '28' on the front, and a diamond-shaped badge at the rear to commemorate the Battle of Alexandria; see Plate 13, *Uniforms of Waterloo*.

The performance of the British infantry in the Peninsular War is legendary. Frequently ill-supplied, usually outnumbered but magnificently led at regimental level, they performed prodigious feats of arms with astonishing regularity; latterly, their conviction of their own invincibility – and that of their commander – produced an unshakeable morale which was second to none. In assessing the most decisive reason for French defeat in the Peninsular War, the British infantry must have one of the strongest cases.

8 BRITAIN:
a) **Officer, Light Company, 45th Foot, 1812.**
b) **Infantry officer in greatcoat, 1810.**

The greatcoated officer is taken from a drawing by Major St Clair; noteworthy are the overalls made from local cloth and the oilskin plume-cover. The greatcoat (of many styles) was so voluminous as to double as a sleeping-bag; Sgt Cooper (among others) noted how both officers and men would put their legs into the sleeves and fasten the greatcoat around them.

The officer of the 45th wears the uniform of light companies of line regiments, characterized by green plume, short jacket, 'wings', corded sash and bugle-horn shako-badge. The latter caused confusion on at least one occasion, when officers of the 32nd at Cadiz were mistaken for bandsmen! The 45th's battalion company officers wore the long-tailed coat with a green-backed, silver figure-of-eight device on the turnbacks, the light company having a silver-embroidered bugle-horn on a green disc. The lapels are shown fastened back to resemble a plastron, the facing-colour usually concealed on campaign. The collar-lace (usually a single loop and button on each side) and chain wings are taken from a contemporary portrait. The officer carries the regulation flank company sabre from the shoulder-belt, the plate of which was oval, bearing an embossed crowned garter with '45' in the centre. Other ranks' lace, in bastion-shaped pairs, had an interwoven green line. Light infantry field officers wore epaulettes *on top* of the wings.

Lieut. Macpherson of the 45th's grenadiers found an unusual use for his jacket at the storming of the San Roque bastion at Badajos; though seriously wounded he fought his way to a tower from which a French flag was flying, hauled it down, and having no British flag to raise hoisted his jacket on the flag-pole! The Sherwood Foresters commemorated this deed by flying a red jacket on the anniversary of Badajos Day (6 April).

9 BRITAIN:
a) **Colour-Sergeant, Grenadier Company, 87th Foot, 1814.**
b) **Corporal, Battalion Company, 1st Foot Guards, undress, 1814.**

The 1812 regulations introduced the felt-bodied, false-fronted 'Belgic' shako for line regiments, its inspiration perhaps the Portuguese 'barretina'; it was worn by officers as well as other ranks, some with neck-covers as in Plate 7. Its use in the Peninsula is doubtful, probably restricted to units or drafts arriving after 1812 and possibly units re-clothed during the war. Plume-colours were unchanged, but a new shako-plate and white cap-cords were introduced, the latter mixed crimson-and-gold for officers and green for some light companies, who from about 1814 sometimes had a bugle-horn badge on the cap.

The rank of colour-sergeant was introduced in July 1813 as a reward of merit; its badge was ultimately a crown over a flag over crossed swords over a single chevron (on three gold chevrons for Guards), with ordinary chevrons on the left arm, though designs varied; Costello of the 95th notes that as no crossed-sword badges had been issued, 'our master-tailor ... formed an imitation with coloured silks worked on the arms of the men appointed'. Some regiments had their own merit-badges, for example the 52nd (see Plate 11), and the 28th which awarded crowns or stars to be worn above the left-arm chevrons. (Defaulters of the 94th had a patch of yellow and black sewn to their sleeves.)

Battalion and grenadier company sergeants wore only one shoulder-belt, as they carried no cartridge-box or musket; other equipment – haversack, knapsack and wooden canteen – was standard. Their arms included straight-bladed swords and the archaic seven-foot spontoon with cross-bar to prevent over-penetration. Cooper of the 7th records a sergeant falling over whilst running with the spontoon, running himself through with the butt-end!

The Guards regiments wore infantry uniform, with blue facings (and flank company wings), gold lace for officers and sergeants and white for other ranks, 'bastion'-shaped for the 1st Guards, pointed in pairs for the 2nd and pointed in threes for the 3rd. The corporal illustrated wears 'undress' uniform used for drill and fatigues, consisting of short-tailed white jacket with regimental facings and forage cap, the design of which varied between regiments; those of the Guards had a white pompom on top for 'battalion', red for grenadier and green for light companies. Apparently this uniform was used for foraging in the Peninsula, Capt. Gronow recording a regimental order which insisted the men 'dress in uniform, [i.e. red] to show the country-people that they belonged to the British army'. Apparently the Guards' first 'Belgic' cap had a brass-

102

bound front (gold lace for officers) but was discontinued in about June 1812.

The superior discipline and *esprit de corps* of the Guards was legendary; at the worst stage of the Corunna retreat, Sir John Moore pointed to a unit marching 'as if in their own barrack-yard', with drums beating and drum-major at the head, twirling his staff; 'Those', said Moore, 'must be the Guards'. Their preoccupation in ensuring as immaculate appearance as possible, however, drew the following rebuke from Wellington near Bayonne: 'Lord Wellington does not approve of the use of umbrellas during the enemy's firing, and will not allow the "gentlemen's sons" to make themselves ridiculous in the eyes of the army.' See also Plates 11, 12 and 13, *Uniforms of Waterloo*.

10 BRITAIN:
a) Piper, 71st (Highland) Light Infantry, 1812.
b) Private, Grenadier Company, 92nd Highlanders, 1814.

The 42nd, 79th and 92nd wore 'Highland' uniform (with bonnet and kilt) in the Peninsular War, and pipers of the 71st retained their traditional dress even after 'de-kilting' and conversion to light infantry in 1809. The 71st should have worn Highland dress in the Corunna campaign, but since returning from South America in December 1807 had worn either tartan 'truibhs' (trews) or grey overalls, with sporrans worn in full dress, receiving an issue of truibhs at Lisbon. Their tartan was McKenzie – the '42nd' or 'Government' sett with red and white lines added. Musicians (not pipers) of the 71st wore 'reversed colours', buff jackets faced red. Other ranks' lace was square-ended, with a red stripe. Apparently no pipe-banners were used, at least one (probably all) being captured at Buenos Aires. Feather bonnets were discontinued for all except pipers in 1809, many having been denuded before then, the feathers being sold to Portuguese ladies! The light infantry head-dress which replaced the bonnet was a dark blue 'stovepipe' shako with diced band at the bottom, probably the previous bonnet blocked into shape; see *Uniforms of Waterloo*, Plate 16. A further link with the Highland tradition was the shoulder-sash worn by officers and sergeants of the 71st.

By 1814 only one of the Highland regiments had any kilts left, the 42nd, though Sgt Anton records that even they were 'beginning to lose it by degrees'. Some men of the 42nd had the kilt made into tartan 'truibhs', and 'TS' of the 71st notes an issue of grey trousers to the 92nd at that time. Apparently some had forsaken the kilt even earlier, Sgt Nicol recording that both he and Sgt MacBean (both 92nd) had portions of their trousers driven into leg-wounds at Talavera. The kilt, in fact, was a mixed blessing; while useful for fanning a camp-fire (hence the nickname 'the Highland man's bellows'), Lieut. Hope of the 92nd tells how a belt of thornbushes at Vittoria cut the legs to pieces.

Regimental distinctions were restricted to facing-colours, lace, and tartan, and smaller ones like the 42nd's famous red plumes (red over white for grenadiers, red over green for light company, red over yellow for drummers). The 42nd had blue facings, 'bastion' loops with a red stripe; the 79th green facings, square-ended loops in pairs with a yellow and two red stripes; the 92nd yellow facings, square-ended loops in pairs with a blue stripe. The 42nd's 'Government' tartan had a red over-stripe for their grenadiers; the 79th wore Cameron of Erracht tartan (basically Macdonald sett minus three red lines, plus a yellow overstripe); and the 92nd the Gordon tartan ('Government' sett with a yellow overstripe). Short gaiters were worn over the hose on campaign, though the private illustrated has Spanish sandals. Officers usually wore overalls except for full dress; sporrans were rarely taken on active service. Standard infantry equipment was carried, though on first disembarking in August 1808 the 71st carried their personal equipment in a rolled blanket. See also *Uniforms of Waterloo*, Plates 16 and 17.

Pipers were only officially sanctioned in 1854, being appointed by the regiment prior to this date; they occasionally wore officers'-pattern uniform minus badges of rank. Invaluable to the morale of a Highland regiment, pipers performed more feats of heroism throughout the war than perhaps any other rank; for example, George Clarke of the 71st received a set of silver pipes for continuing to play at Vimiero though seriously wounded. Apparently some non-Highland units also had (unofficial) pipers, Lt-Col. Steevens of the 20th lamenting the loss of 'our poor Scotch piper' at Roncevalles.

11 **BRITAIN:**
   a) Officer, 52nd Light Infantry, 1813.
   b) Officer, 43rd Light Infantry, 1812.

With training developed by Sir John Moore, and inspired by 'Black Bob' Craufurd, the British Light Brigade, later Division, was the finest light infantry formation of the Napoleonic Wars, a genuine élite comprising at various times elements of the 43rd, 52nd, 95th, 1st and 3rd Caçadores and 17th and 20th Portuguese Line.

The light infantry uniform was distinguished by the bugle-horn badge and green plume on the 'stovepipe' cap (the 'Belgic' shako was never adopted) and wings worn by all companies. Light Infantry facing-colours were: 43rd white, other ranks' lace with one red and one black line; 52nd grass-green, lace with a green line; 52nd buff, lace with one red and two blue lines; 68th bottle-green, lace with a red and a green line; 85th yellow, lace with a red zigzag, all lace square-ended, in pairs. Officers of the 43rd adopted unofficial scarlet pelisses, though the term can be misleading, being also applied to the braided overcoat, probably the 'undress pelisse' mentioned by Lieut. Gleig of the 85th. Typical of the 43rd's preoccupation with elegant costume was Capt. Hobkirk, who reputedly spent £1,000 a year on his uniforms, and on being captured in 1813 was mistaken for a general by Marshal Soult! There exists an officer's shako – originally owned by Lieut. Kershaw – which has cords, chinscales and turban, a non-regulation pattern perhaps worn with the pelisse. (The hussar style could have been completed by the adoption of a dolman though the jacket is shown.)

Constantly in the forefront of the war, the Light Division's uniforms became so ragged that the 43rd marched into France wearing trousers made out of blankets and caps 'distorted by alternate rain and sunshine, as well as having served as pillows and nightcaps ... assumed the most monstrous and grotesque shapes' (Capt. Cooke). Nevertheless, the remains of shakos, shoes, knapsacks and canteen-straps were often blackened with soot scraped from the bottom of camp-kettles when ordinary blacking was unavailable. Lieut. Grattan describes the 43rd *en route* to assault the breach at Badajos: '... in the highest spirits ... had no knapsacks – their firelocks were slung over their shoulders – their shirt-collars were open, and there was an indescribable *something* about them that impressed the lookers-on with admiration and awe ...'

The officer of the 52nd is taken from a St Clair sketch; officers often carried small knapsacks, as Gleig records: 'I ... stuck my pistols in a black leathern haversack, which ... usually hung at my back'. A regimental distinction noted by Costello was a laurel-wreath badge worn on the right arm, with the letters vs beneath, signifying 'Valiant Stormer', awarded to survivors of the 'forlorn hopes' of Badajos and Ciudad Rodrigo. It is interesting to note that Standing Orders of the 85th (1813) record that musket-barrels were to be browned, 'never to be rubbed with any rough substance', presumably to reduce the tell-tale flash of sun on polished metal.

12 BRITAIN:
a) **Officer, 95th Rifles, campaign uniform, 1810–12.**
b) **Bugler, 95th Rifles, 1808.**
c) **Officer, 95th Rifles, 1811.**

Formed in 1800, the 95th Rifles were the origin of the modern infantry tactic; experienced marksmen trained to operate as individuals, expert in skirmishing, scouting and outpost duty. A highly-disciplined, fast-moving élite, the 95th's status was indicated by their unique 'rifle-green' uniform (a rudimentary camouflage) and their accurate 'Baker' rifled muskets. Their matchless *esprit de corps* provoked a flood of reminiscences from the pens of ex-members of 'The Sweeps', a regimental nickname taken from their sombre uniforms.

The 95th's 'Peninsular' dress has been illustrated frequently (see *Uniforms of Waterloo*, Plate 18), so three less-common examples are shown. The officer in pelisse is after a sketch from life of Capt. E. Kent, made during the war, showing the officers' hussar-dress of dolman, pelisse, corded sash and 'sugar-loaf' cap with folding, square-cut peak, plus privately-acquired overalls with a black stripe on the outer seam. Kent carries the 'half-moon sabre' described by Kincaid as 'better designed to shave a lady's-maid than a Frenchman's head'.

The bugler is taken from a water-colour of c. 1804, showing basic other ranks' uniform, plus interesting features: square-cut shako-peak and no bugle-horn badge, and white edging to facings and shoulder-straps. Equipment was of black leather, including waist-belt with 'S'-clasp, small powder-flask and a white roll on top of the knapsack. The 'Baker' rifle is shown in Plate 13. In addition to ordinary chevrons, N.C.O.s had a white sword-badge on the right upper arm (if acting in superior rank); 'chosen men' wore a ring of white lace on the right arm and (in 1800) 'marksmen' wore green cockades and 'ordinary riflemen' white. Sergeants' sashes were scarlet with central black stripe, Harris recording the sergeant-major's full dress: '... quite a beau ... a sling belt to his sword like a field-officer, a tremendous green feather in his cap, a flaring sash, his whistle and powder-flask displayed, an officer's pelisse over one shoulder ...' The whistle, carried by officers and N.C.O.s, was used for signalling in the field.

The officer in campaign uniform is reconstructed from the letters of Lieut. George Simmons, who described his costume in 1810–11, typically tattered: 'My jacket is brown instead of green. Never was seen such a motley group of fellows ... I am a perfect guerrilla, having broken my sword, lost my sash, and am as ragged as a sweep ...' In addition to a jacket of local cloth, the officer has a 'linc' pattern sash, Simmons having exchanged sashes with his brother, in the 34th; the bottom of his overalls were burnt whilst drying over a camp-fire! Without wearing captured French items, Simmons noted, 'I should be nearly naked'. In addition to a knapsack taken from a man he killed at Talavera, he took a cloak off a dead Frenchman in 1813 and still indulged in corpse-robbing at Waterloo.

Numerous reminiscences record the deterioration of uniforms, for example Kincaid: the jacket in 'shreds and patches ... woe befell the regimental small-clothes ...' (1810); Rifleman Costello: '... fierce embrowned visages, covered with whisker and mustachio ... our clothing patched and of all colours ...' (1811), 'green having become by far the least conspicuous colour in the regiment' (1812); Rifleman Harris, after the Corunna retreat: 'in a ghastly state ... feet swathed in bloody rags, clothing that hardly covered their nakedness, accoutrements in shreds ... arms nearly useless ... officers ... in as miserable a plight ...'; at this time Rifleman Green wore a stolen general's hat! After the capture of Ciudad Rodrigo the dress was so motley that even Wellington had to enquire who they were: '... scarcely a vestige of uniform among the men, some of whom were dressed in Frenchmen's coats, some in white breeches and huge jack-boots, some with cocked hats ... most of their swords ... stuck full of hams, tongues, and loaves of bread ... there never was a better masked corps ...' (Kincaid); '... in all varieties imaginable, some with jackboots on, others with frock-coats, epaulettes ...' (Costello); 'some ... in priests' or friars' garments – some appeared in female dresses, as nuns, etc. ... whimsical and fantastical figures' (Surtees).

The most bizarre costume was that worn from choice rather than necessity, be it Kincaid's 'donkey-load of pistols in my belt, to impress the natives', the exaggerated hussar uniform, or the dressing-gown, nightcap and slippers worn by Col. Beckwith in the action of Barba del Puerco in March 1810! The 95th excelled at such 'outpost duty' which revealed French manoeuvres, concealed Allied activity and required 'a clear head, bold heart and a clean pair of heels' (Kincaid). The 95th's contribution to the French defeat in the Peninsula – and ultimately in the remainder of Europe – is incalculable.

13 BRITAIN:
a) **Private, 5th Battalion, 60th (Royal American) Regt, 1812.**
b) **Officer, 5th Battalion, 60th (Royal American) Regt, 1814.**

Raised in the colonies as the Royal American Regiment in 1755, the 60th Foot was a conventional line regiment until in 1797 the remnants of the French *émigré* and German mercenary corps in British service were formed into battalions of rifles and light infantry. The 5th and 6th Battns, 60th, were raised from this source and uniformed in green, the 5th serving in the Peninsula as detached companies, in a rôle like the 95th. So German was its original composition that the term 'Jägers' (anglicized into the nickname 'The Jaggers') was used unofficially. By the end of the war drafts of British had reduced the German element to less than half, with only nine German officers. The unit's worth was recognized by Wellington's General Order recommending the detached companies 'to the particular care of the officers commanding the brigades to which they have been attached: they will find them to be most useful, active and brave troops . . .'

The officer illustrated, principally after Cremer, wears a dolman; some sources show short-tailed jackets with the buttons set closer together on the breast, and less braid. Among other details recorded by contemporary sources is a list of clothing belonging to Lt-Col. Fitzgerald of the 5th Battn in 1814, hussar uniform including 'pelisse of green, sable fur, royal cord breast and fully trimmed', 'green sash, scarlet barrels' instead of the light infantry version illustrated, a 'blue long pelisse' (the braided frock-coat), blue overalls, blue 'ornamented pantaloons', white full dress pantaloons 'full trimmed', black pouch bearing silver bugle, black belts with plated fittings and steel sabre with black scabbard, and shako with square-cut peak, and 'black silk line twice around, two tassels, silver bugle'. Traditionally the regimental Maltese Cross badge was taken from that of Hompesch's Chasseurs (a German corps drafted into the 60th), but its use at this time is uncertain, though shown in a miniature of Capt. Wolff.

The Private (after C. H. Smith) wears the red-faced regimental uniform and blue breeches (perhaps piped red) and carries the 'Baker' rifle and sword-bayonet with stirrup-hilt. On campaign the uniforms deteriorated so much that in May 1809 the 5th Battn's commanding officer allowed his men to cut off the skirts of their jackets to patch what remained!

14 BRITAIN:
a) **Corporal, Royal Artillery, 1808.**
b) **Quartermaster, Royal Horse Artillery, 1814**

The light dragoon-style Royal Horse Artillery uniform included the 'Tarleton' helmet and braided dolman. The Quartermaster illustrated is taken from a portrait of James Wightman, showing variations including an officer-style sash and laced shoulder-straps. Officers had gold lace and other ranks yellow, possibly excepting senior N.C.O.s. The helmet had a white plume on the left-hand side for full dress, and a turban of either black or dark blue. Hamilton Smith shows a gunner with similar shabraque, but smaller and edged red, the fur confined to holster-caps.

Overalls were commonly worn on campaign, usually grey with one or two scarlet stripes. Contemporary sources show the Corps of Drivers, Royal Artillery, wearing either Foot Artillery jackets with Horse Artillery helmet and overalls, or Horse Artillery uniform and plain jackets with three rows of buttons on the breast; see *Uniforms of Waterloo*, Plates 8/9. Officers adopted certain non-regulation styles; Capt. Norman Ramsey (who saved his guns at Fuentes de Oñoro by charging through French cavalry) preferred a light cavalry belt instead of a sash, while Capt. Thomas Dyneley ordered from London a patent sabretache, with ink-stand, lock, key and 'two knots'. The pelisse, unofficially adopted by officers, was originally a 'poor shabby concern' according to Capt. Mercer, trimmed with brown fur. It became more ornate with grey astrakhan edging and either gold or black mohair braid, its use in the Peninsula confirmed by an 1812 portrait of Capt. Richard Bogue. An order of January 1812 authorizing the use of 'a short surtout ... to be worn as a pelisse on service' probably referred to a braided frock-coat.

Royal Foot Artillery uniforms followed infantry patterns, but dark blue with scarlet facings and yellow 'bastion' lace (gold for officers), with 'stovepipe', later 'Belgic', shako bearing white plume and distinctive plate. White breeches and black gaiters, and white or grey overalls, were usually worn, but yellow-laced blue breeches and half-gaiters are shown by Atkinson (1807). The corporal (after Atkinson) wears cross-belts supporting a white leather pouch (bearing a brass crowned-garter plate after Hamilton Smith, though perhaps the crown-on-red-patch badge was used earlier in the war); a red flask-cord and brass vent-unblocker were worn on the belt. At least one R.A. officer changed his uniform for reasons of diplomacy; Capt. Alexander Dickson was appointed field commander of Wellington's artillery on the strength of his lieutenant-colonelcy in the Portuguese army, and always wore a shabby Portuguese uniform so as not to give offence to his subordinates who far outranked him in the Royal Artillery!

15 **BRITAIN:**
   a) **Private, Royal Sappers and Miners, 1814.**
   b) **Officer, Royal Engineers, 1814.**

Lack of trained engineers was the most serious deficiency in Wellington's army; as late as April 1812 he reported that 'equipped as we are, the British army are not capable of carrying on a regular siege'. The Royal Engineers was a corps of officers directed by the Board of Ordnance, 'all ... inherent pomp and acquired gravity' (Blakeney) of whom no more than about thirty served in the field, commanded by the able Major Richard Fletcher until his death in 1813. The Corps of Royal Military Artificers was composed of sergeants and other ranks who were responsible for directing the untrained troops and civilian labourers who performed the actual task of construction; in 1809 there were only two such sergeants and twenty-seven men with Wellington, augmented in 1811 by two more sergeants and fifty-seven men 'who had never seen a sap, battery, or trench'. A needed re-organization in 1812 expanded the corps, improved training, and changed the title to 'Royal Military Artificers or Sappers and Miners', becoming 'Royal Sappers and Miners' in 1813, when some 300 were serving in the Peninsula. So poor was the organization that any credit for successful sieges and the construction of the Lines of Torres Vedras belongs to the individual R.E. officers, who suffered severely; for example, of the twenty-one present at the first siege of Badajos, only five came through the war unscathed.

Until 1812 R.E. officers wore dark blue coatees with black facings and gold epaulettes, but no lace, with white-plumed bicorns and either breeches or overalls, a uniform which frequently attracted unwanted attention from French snipers and British sentries; 'A Subaltern' writing in the *United Service Journal* (1831) noted how he mistook Engineer Capt. Patten for a Frenchman during a night reconnaissance at Badajos due to his dark uniform. In 1812 the Engineer uniform became scarlet with 'Garter blue' facings, the design of gold lace illustrated taken from a portrait of Major Fletcher by J. Barwell, which shows the lapels fastened back to display a blue plastron-front. See also *Uniforms of Waterloo*, Plate 19.

The Royal Military Artificers wore dark blue with red facings, shako with white plume and (in 1801) a 'working dress' of blue cloth jacket and blue serge pantaloons, and were armed with swords (and perhaps muskets, as issued to the Walcheren Expedition's artificers). Veterans of Egypt were allowed to wear the sphinx device on their appointments. The Royal Sappers and Miners wore scarlet infantry uniform, with dark blue facings and yellow 'bastion' lace, grey overalls for service (sometimes with red stripe and line of brass buttons), and 'Belgic' cap with yellow cords and white plume. The 'working dress' illustrated consisted of short single-breasted red jacket with dark blue collar and cuffs and no lace, and leather undress cap with semi-circular back and front and brass letters RS&M on the front, and (for trench-work) blue-grey canvas 'breastplate' strapped at the back, and a head-cover made of the same material, folded lengthwise and sewn at the end, like a coalman's traditional head-guard. N.C.O.s wore yellow chevrons on the right arm; a further distinction was a bastion-shaped loop and button on each side of the collar. Weapons varied, with no regulation issue; there are records of pikes and blunderbusses in addition to the short sword. Some companies had individual distinctions, like the grey overalls with black stripe and grey cloth forage-caps trimmed with black braid and bearing the brass initials on the left-hand side worn by those at Cadiz. Rectangular brass buckles were generally used in place of shoulder-belt plates.

16 BRITAIN:
a) **Officer with Colour, Provisional Battn de Roll-Dillon.**
b) **Officer, Light Company, Chasseurs Britanniques, 1812.**

One of the 'foreign corps' of the British army, the Chasseurs Britanniques was formed in 1801 from French *émigrés*, by 1811 including many ex-prisoners of war and deserters, Italians, Poles and Swiss. Officers were mainly French royalists who hated the Bonaparte régime and whose efforts alone made the Chasseurs into a reasonable fighting unit, commended by Wellington for steadiness at Fuentes de Oñoro (but when forming ladder-parties at the storm of Badajos threw their burdens away and fled)! Their desertion record was severe; arriving in the Peninsula in 1811 they lost 139 men in that year, 171 in 1812 and 224 in 1813, including a platoon of two corporals and 16 men deserting *en masse* in October 1812, all Italians save for one Swiss and one Croat. As many of the rank and file had only enlisted in the hopes of deserting back to the French, they were never allowed on outpost duty. They wore infantry uniform with light blue facings, lace silver for officers and white with light blue and red stripes for others. One portrait shows an officer with a red collar; that illustrated wears light company distinctions, bugle-horn badges on turnbacks and wings, and flank company sabre; battalion company officers wore the usual epaulettes and bicorn. Discrepancies of uniform probably existed within the unit, for Wellington enquired of the commanding officer in February 1811, regarding recruits arrived from Gibraltar, 'in what mode' he intended 'to clothe and equip them for service'. The Chasseurs Britanniques should not be confused with the wretched companies of 'Independent Foreigners' who committed every conceivable outrage in the descent on Chesapeake Bay.

The Swiss 'foreign corps' were among the best troops of the British army. The provisional battalion formed from three battalion companies of de Roll's Regt and five companies of Dillon's (named in despatches of 1813 as 'Roll Dillon's'), though not entirely Swiss in composition, was reported to be superior even to the King's German Legion, and served with distinction in eastern Spain in 1813, de Roll's rifle company forming part of a combined light infantry battalion. Both de Roll's and Dillon's wore standard infantry uniform with light blue and golden-yellow facings respectively. Unusual distinctions of de Roll's included silver officers' lace with tasselled ends, other ranks' white lace with tufted ends and a blue stripe (in pairs), red-over-white plumes for battalion companies and belt-plates bearing the Masonic eye device. The rifle company wore green faced black, with white-edged wings and 'Belgic' shako with green cords and plume and white metal bugle-horn badge; a watercolour of an officer shows a 'stovepipe' cap bearing a sphinx badge, and a jacket with ten lines of black braid and three rows of silver buttons.

S. M. Milne illustrates an unusual Colour, bearing the Masonic eye within a Garter inscribed 'Schwebe über uns und segne unsere Treue', with crowned Royal cypher above and a sphinx and wreath below. Combining the facing-colour of Dillon's and the badges of de Roll's, it was probably carried by the provisional battalion.

17 BRITAIN:
a) **Officer, 2nd Dragoons, King's German Legion, campaign dress, 1810.**
b) **Officer, 2nd Dragoons, King's German Legion, drill order, 1810.**

When Hanover was over-run in 1803, King George III (as Elector of Hanover) authorized the formation of a King's German Regiment, of Hanoverian citizens, as part of the British army. So many volunteered that it was expanded into the King's German Legion, eventually comprising eight infantry and two light infantry battalions, five cavalry regiments, horse and foot artillery. Among the finest units of the British Army, the Legion served with great distinction in the Peninsula and at Waterloo.

The two Dragoon and three Light Dragoon regiments were converted in 1813 to Light Dragoons and Hussars respectively. Uniformed in British style, the Light Dragoons initially wore the 'Tarleton' and the 1st apparently a blue 'kollet' (frock-coat) with red facings; hussar dress was adopted in 1813–14 when the Dragoons, becoming 'Light', took British 1812-pattern uniform. See *Uniforms of Waterloo*, Plates 20 and 21.

The Dragoon uniform prior to 1813 is shown in a number of illustrations painted by or under the direction of L.v. Hugo, an officer of the 2nd Dragoons from 1806–16. The officer in campaign dress (based on a Hugo figure entitled 'Officer coming from Lissabon [*sic*] to the Army of the Duke of Wellington') wears British dragoon uniform with large chinscales on the bicorn, the plume in a waterproof cover, gilt shoulder-scales on the blue-faced coatee, leather-booted overalls and simple horse-furniture with fur-covered holster-caps. Another figure shows the bicorn worn 'athwart', with no chinscales but white-over-red plume, and long dark blue greatcoat with a single row of gilt buttons and an elbow-length cape. The officer 'in common drill order' wears an unusual shako with busby-bag, frock-coat, full dress breeches and long boots. The full dress pouch-belt was gold-laced, the black pouch with gilt edging and lion-on-crown badge within a Garter; the white leather undress pouch-belt had a black pouch with gilt lion-on-crown badge. An officer 'dressed for Common Mess days' shown by Hugo wears the undress shako, a scarlet regimental jacket minus collar-lace, worn open to expose the waistcoat, dark blue breeches and 'Hessian' boots. Knötel shows troopers in similar uniform, with yellow lace and scarlet wings with lace edging.

The K.G.L. Dragoons won their greatest fame at Garcia Hernandez (1812), when they broke French infantry in 'square' formation, an outstanding feat which cost the Legion 54 dead and 62 wounded to about 200 French casualties and 1,400 prisoners.

18 BRITAIN:
a) **Officer, Battalion Company, 1st Line Battn, King's German Legion, 1811.**
b) **Assistant-Surgeon, 5th Line Battn, King's German Legion, 1813.**

K.G.L. Line Battns wore British infantry uniform, with blue facings, gold officers' lace, and plain white lace for other ranks. The 1st, 2nd, 4th, 5th, 6th and 7th Line served in the Peninsula with such distinction that the 5th was nicknamed 'The Fighting Battalion' by the British. Highly-trained and efficient (despite the influx of non-German 'foreigners' into the ranks), each line battalion included a half-company of sharpshooters in addition to the usual light company. The two Light Battns wore green 'rifle uniform' with black facings; see *Uniforms of Waterloo*, Plate 23.

The officer illustrated, based on a St Clair drawing, wears non-regulation overalls and light cavalry sabre worn from a waist-belt like a field officer. The coatee is from an extant example, double-breasted with eight square-ended gold loops on the front. The turn-back-badges were diamond-shaped, edged gold and bearing a gold-embroidered crown over KGL over a laurel-spray. See *Uniforms of Waterloo*, Plate 22.

The Assistant-Surgeon wears the single-breasted uniform of all British medical officers, but with lace loops instead of the usual embroidered dummy-loops. The German-style undress cap was not restricted to the Legion; St Clair, for example, shows a British officer wearing a similar item (apparently with waterproof cover) at Fuentes de Oñoro. All infantry surgeons wore a black plume in the hat (the 'Belgic' shako was adopted in 1812), and a light-bladed sword on a waist-belt, usually black leather. Various haversacks were used on campaign; 'D.B.', a surgeon writing in the *United Service Journal* (1831), describes his equipment at Salamanca: '... a pair of capacious "Alforges", or Spanish saddle-bags, containing, on one side, a plentiful supply of the minor apparatus of surgery, and on the other, "provent" ... Suspended on my saddle-bow was a "borachio", or leathern bag, of country wine'.

Lieut. Edmund Wheatley of the 5th Line Battn sketched (presumably) men of his battalion in October 1813, wearing pale yellow (faded white?) tail-less undress jackets with red collar and cuffs and no lace, grey overalls and peakless red undress caps edged around the top with white lace and apparently six lines of lace on the crown, intersecting in the centre. Wheatley noted his battalion using white blankets: 'I rolled myself in the Sergeant's blanket ... A violent kick in the neck awoke me suddenly and the Colonel's voice of "What's this white thing?"'.

19 BRITAIN:
a) **Private, Loyal Lusitanian Legion, 1809.**
b) **Jäger, Brunswick Oels Corps, 1812.**
c) **Private, Rifle Company, Calabrian Free Corps, 1812.**

The Duke of Brunswick's 'Black Legion' (raised in 1809 for Austrian service) transferred to British in August 1809. Twelve infantry companies (including probably three of Jägers) served with Wellington, and a hussar detachment in eastern Spain. Recruited from ex-prisoners of war and assorted foreigners (Germans, Croats, Danes, Dutch, Italians and Poles) the desertion-rate was severe, Leach of the 95th remarking that 'we had a lease of them but for a few weeks'. In August 1813 Wellington noted that no fewer than ninety had deserted in the 'last few days', whilst Craufurd told them 'that if any of these gentlemen have a wish to go over to the enemy, let them express it, and I give my word of honour I will grant them a pass to that effect instantly, for we are better without such'. The familiar black Brunswick uniform with black-plumed shako and braided jacket faced light blue (see *Uniforms of Waterloo*, Plates 30–31) was not worn by the Jägers, who wore the green illustrated (after Goddard & Booth), with infantry shako bearing large white metal skull and crossed bones badge, which Costello notes earned the nickname 'death and glory men', 'dressed in dark green, which but too frequently enabled them to steal past the French'; Goddard shows the painted knapsack with the motto NUNQUAM RETRORSUM. The hussars wore the same shako, and black dolman faced light blue.

The Loyal Lusitanian Legion was a 'foreign corps' of three infantry battalions, a dragoon regiment and six guns, raised in London and Oporto, paid by the British Treasury and commanded by Sir Robert Wilson, with sixty-five British and thirty-five Portuguese officers, and Portuguese other ranks. Initially of fine quality, the Legion acted independently in semi-guerrilla actions, gaining a fine reputation in 1809–10 (on at least one raid the infantry was mounted on horses and mules). The replacement of the independent Wilson marked a decline in quality until Wellington reported it 'a miserable body of men' by February 1811, transferring to Portuguese service as the 7th, 8th and 9th Caçadores. The infantry wore British dark green 'rifle' uniform (probably with white overalls for summer), though smaller details are in doubt, limited to early drawings and an uncertain reproduction uniform. Though the Portuguese 'stovepipe' cap used to be thought the head dress, it seems from extant caps that the 'Barretina' with plate embossed LLL was worn at least initially. Sources show either two cross-belts or one and a waistbelt. The Dragoons or 'light horse' wore green faced white and the artillery green faced black. One battalion was apparently designated light infantry, Beresford referring to 'the light battalion L.L. legion' in May 1811.

The Calabrian Free Corps was raised by Sir John Stuart in Sicily, with British senior officers and all other ranks Calabrians. Goddard & Booth show a private in the blue-green jacket illustrated, with unusual lacing on the breast, and an officer (see Black-and-White Plate 'A') is scarlet faced yellow and sky-blue breeches. Goddard notes 'The clothing and appointments ... of light infantry and rifle corps'; probably the corps was composed of part light infantry (in red) and part rifles. It served in eastern Spain in 1812–13, latterly as part of the 'advance corps' with the 4th K.G.L. Line Battn and de Roll's rifle company. Contemporary despatches refer to the unit as the

'Calabrese free corps' or 'Calabrian light infantry and rifles'.

20 PORTUGAL:
a) Staff Officer, 1811.
b) General.

The General Officer in Portuguese staff uniform is based on actual garments recorded by C. A. Norman in *Tradition*. The red-and-blue national cockade is worn on the hat, and rank indicated by silver leaf-embroidery on collar and cuffs; turnback-badges consisted of silver crowned-heart devices on blue backing. General officers are also shown with gold lace, dark blue breeches and long boots, and plain breeches and black belts for undress. The red sash – here with silver tassels – was worn by all Portuguese officers.

The staff officer wears Portuguese uniform, modified according to the letters of William Warre of the British 23rd Light Dragoons, from 1809 A.D.C. to Marshal Beresford and a major in the Portuguese Army (Lt-Col. from 1811). Much of his uniform came from Britain, the Portuguese regulations being only loosely interpreted. The hat, for example, he thought 'tawdry, and such as I would not wear'; a new hat ordered 'must have handsome round Staff "tawsels" and ribbons at the sides, but must not be gold laced, as the new regulation is . . . I suppose our good chiefs do not think our Generals or Staff get killed off fast enough that they order them cocked hats with gold binding. It must only be meant for Wimbledon. There are no Voltigeurs there, and a gold laced cocked hat, though very ugly, is a very harmless thing – not here'. The hat is shown covered by an oilskin 'waterproof'. The dark blue coatee with white piping and gold embroidery was worn under an overcoat, Warre bemoaning his coat which 'gets so soon wet, is so heavy when filled with water, and takes so many days drying ... of little use on horseback, as it does not cover the knees ... a cloak lined with warm but light stuff is much better ... I have latterly practised riding in an oil skin cape over my great coat ...' His sabre is British, the Portuguese issue 'of wretched quality and badly finished ... I am vexed at it, for the prices are for the best'. He also wears his 'white Dragoon sword-belt' and 'long Regency boots' ordered in September 1808.

The surgeon who attended Beresford at Salamanca records the uniforms worn at that battle; Warre had Portuguese staff uniform, but Beresford was dressed in 'a blue frock-coat and white waistcoat', apparently civilian. Even Warre apparently wore a British A.D.C.'s coat at times, for everyday wear, 'as I ... do not wish to make another Portuguese, which is very expensive ...'

21 PORTUGAL:
a) Trooper, 3rd Cavalry, 1809.
b) Officer, 10th Cavalry, 1812.

The Portuguese cavalry was the least efficient branch of the army, some regiments never becoming effective or even all mounted (the 2nd, 3rd and 12th were utilized as dismounted garrison troops). No more than 1,300 of the 7,128 establishment strength were ever fit for field duty at any one time. Regimental strength rarely approached

300 (establishment 590), the 4th and 10th serving in 1811 with only 450 between them. Brigadier William Cox reported the garrison cavalry at Almeida 'in the most wretched state ... only a burthen to the country without being of the slightest use. The best of the horses are mere skin and bone, and are incapable of performing any kind of service'. On occasion, however, they behaved well: Warre noted the 1st Regt behaving 'most nobly' in July 1810, and D'Urban's 1st and 11th fought well at Salamanca but bolted at Majadahonda (11 August 1811), of which D'Urban reported: 'My poor fellows are still a most ... uncertain sort of fighting people. At Salamanca they followed me like British dragoons; yesterday they ... went just far enough to land me in the enemy's ranks ... vanished before the French helmets like leaves before the autumn wind. They require ... incentive of shouts, and the inspiring cheers of a British line ... they will never be quite safe by themselves'. Wellington's comment: 'Worse than useless'.

Regulation uniform included fur-crested leather helmet with brass fittings and plate bearing a cut-out regimental number, and jacket with the following distinctions:

Regt	Collar/Cuffs	Piping	Regt	Collar/Cuffs	Piping
1st (Alcantara)	white	white	7th (Lisbon)	yellow	white
2nd (Moura)	white	red	8th (Elvas)	yellow	red
3rd (Olivenca)	white	yellow	9th (Chaves)	yellow	yellow
4th (Principe)	red	white	10th (Santarem)	light blue	white
5th (Evora)	red	red	11th (Almeida)	light blue	red
6th (Braganca)	red	yellow	12th (Miranda)	light blue	yellow

The officer of the 10th is from Denis Dighton, showing an unusual uniform and shako. Dighton may be in error, but the uniform is probably an example of non-regulation dress adopted by some officers, or an 'issued' uniform in a time of scarcity of regulation patterns.

22 PORTUGAL:
a) **Sergeant, 18th Infantry.**
b) **Officer, 21st Infantry, with Colour.**

Each Portuguese infantry regiment consisted of two battalions (the 21st only one), and each battalion of (probably) five centre, one grenadier and one light company, though apparently the light companies were detached about 1811; battalion establishment was 770 of all ranks, often less on campaign.

1806-regulation uniform included the 'barretina' cap, with lower plate bearing the regimental number and higher plate the Portuguese arms. Plumes were white, the bow-cockade red-and-blue for all ranks, and cords of mixed blue and the facing-colour with gold thread woven in for corporals and above. Some sources show the jacket worn by officers instead of the long-tailed coatee. Blue shoulder-straps with facing-coloured piping were worn by privates and corporals, and scaled straps by higher ranks. Grenadiers had epaulette-fringes of mixed blue and facing-colour, and brass grenade-badge on the shako below the Portuguese arms; pioneers had crossed axes in this place. Dark blue breeches with short gaiters were worn in winter, and either one-piece white 'gaiter-trousers' or loose white overalls in summer, though varied colours were adopted on campaign; officers had 'Hessian' or top-boots. Equipment consisted of hide knapsacks and cartridge-box bearing brass regimental number, though British patterns were also issued; sabres were apparently initially confined to the N.C.O.s and probably grenadiers, spreading to all ranks by about 1810. British muskets were widely-used.

Rank-distinctions were: Colonel, two shoulder-scales with bullions; Lt-Col., as Col. but bullion on right only; Major, as Col. but bullions on left; Capt., scales with fringes; Lieut., as Lt-Col. but with fringe; 2nd Lieut. as Major, but fringe; Sergeant, scales with yellow fringe; 2nd Sgt, as Sgt but fringe on right only; 'Furriel' as Sgt with fringe on left; Corpl, two yellow stripes around cuff; Lance-Corpl, one stripe.

Facing-colours are shown in the table.

Regt	Collar	Cuffs	Piping & Turnbacks
1st (la Lippe)	blue	white	white
2nd (Lagos)	blue	white	red
3rd (1st Olivenca)	blue	white	yellow
4th (Freire)	blue	red	white
5th (1st Elvas)	blue	red	red
6th (1st Oporto)	blue	red	yellow
7th (Setubal)	blue	yellow	white
8th (Evora)	blue	yellow	red
9th (Viana)	blue	yellow	yellow
10th (Lisbon)	blue	light blue	white
11th (1st Almeida)	blue	light blue	red
12th (Chaves)	blue	light blue	yellow
13th (Peniche)	white	white	white
14th (Tavira)	white	white	red
15th (2nd Olivenca)	white	white	yellow
16th (Viera Telles)	red	red	white
17th (2nd Elvas)	red	red	red
18th (2nd Oporto)	red	red	yellow
19th (Cascaes)	yellow	yellow	white
20th (Campomayor)	yellow	yellow	red
21st (Valenca)	yellow	yellow	yellow
22nd (Serpa)	light blue	light blue	white
23rd (2nd Almeida)	light blue	light blue	red
24th (Braganca)	light blue	light blue	yellow

The elaborate flag bore the central motto JULGARIES QUALHE MAS EXCELENTE SE SERDO MUNDO REI DE TAL GENTE, and the regimental number below the coat-of-arms.

23 PORTUGAL:
a) **Private, 20th Infantry.**
b) **Corporal, Light Company, 4th Infantry, 1811.**
c) **Private, Algarve Volunteers.**

The Light Company corporal wears the 'stovepipe' cap which replaced the 'barretina' c. 1810–11, with plate as before. Note light infantry distinctions of bugle-horn badge and green fringe on the uniquely-Portuguese shoulder-strap/wings. The private of the 20th is from Denis Dighton, showing a cap-plate with embossed number, circular cockade, plume in British colouring, ribbon-chinstrap tied up on the shako, and brass shoulder-scales, probably not signifying N.C.O. rank but perhaps worn by all. Equipment includes a British-style belt-plate and civilian leather wine-bottle. Warre reported in February 1810 that 'I never saw a Regt embark in better style or higher spirits than the 20th ... did for Cadiz a few days ago. They embarked 1,400 strong, and lost only 6 deserted, which does them and their country great honour ...'

One of numerous irregular forces, the Algarve volunteer wears a semi-civilian 'uniform' of peasant cloth, variously shown by different authorities, a reproduction of uncertain authenticity having white facings.

The 'ordenanca', a '*levée en masse*' of the peasantry, was a relic of the middle ages and of limited value. Without uniforms and armed only with agricultural tools and sharpened vine-poles, they acted as guerrillas, harrying the flanks of an enemy, as they did to Masséna in 1810. Almost bereft of firearms, the ordenanca were, at best, of 'nuisance value'; those captured were shot as 'brigands' by the French, French prisoners being murdered in retaliation.

24 PORTUGAL:
a) **Officer, 18th Militia.**
b) **Private, 18th Militia.**
c) **Private, Militia.**

Each 'Division' of Portugal (North, Centre and South) was supposed to provide sixteen Militia regiments, named after towns, of two battalions each (most had only one), each battalion of six companies. Though occasionally in action (for example the Tomar Militia which ran away at Busaco), their main use was for garrison duty, releasing regular troops; as Wellington wrote in February 1811, 'The greater number of this description of men we have, the greater number of the better description we should have to dispose of.' Apart from duty on the lines of Torres Vedras, Wellington ordered the militia not to fight if possible, which officers like Col. Trant disobeyed to find the militia bolting as at Guarda when whole brigades fled before a small French force.

The 18th (Vila do Conde) Militia illustrated wear the 1806-pattern infantry uniform. Denis Dighton shows a more conventional blue uniform with brass shoulder-scales, plain shako, and very rudimentary equipment, the 'knapsack' apparently a bundle wrapped in a blanket. Discipline and equipment was often wretched. In April 1809 Trant reported his troops – expected to hold the Vouga River against Soult – as consisting of 200 students and 1,100 Coimbra Militia, 'in the worst possible state', never having fired a musket and so badly equipped that 600 had only pikes, and officers 'totally incompetent to keep order'. Brigadier Cox of the Almeida garrison reported his Militia with no accoutrements, carrying cartridges in their pockets, a highly dangerous practice. One of his units mutinied for being unpaid for eleven months, the colonel having diverted the money into his own pocket – though he could not be dismissed as the regiment's two lieutenant-colonels were his nephews, and children!

25 PORTUGAL:
a) Private, 4th Caçadores, 1812.
b) Private, 1st Caçadores, 1809.

The Caçadores ('hunters' in Portuguese) were among the best of Wellington's allies. Raised in November 1808 as six light infantry battalions, they were increased to twelve in 1811 by the transfer from British service of the Loyal Lusitanian Legion and the creation of new corps. Trained by British officers, they were the equivalent of the British 5/60th and 95th.

Initially, the infantry-style uniform was a distinctive dark brown, piped dark green; all wore yellow loops on the breast. Facing-colours (on collar and cuffs) were: 1st (Castello de Vide) and 4th (Vizeu) Regts, light blue; 2nd (Moura) and 5th (Campomayor) red; 3rd (Villa Real) and 6th (Oporto) yellow; the 1st, 2nd and 3rd had brown collars. The 'barretina' shako was of line pattern, save for the plate (bearing the regimental number in the 'curl' of a hunting-horn) and green plume (black for '*atiradores*' or sharpshooter company, who had green-fringed shoulder-straps). Musicians had green-and-yellow or green-and-white lace on collar and cuffs.

In about 1811 a new uniform was introduced, consisting of a 'stovepipe' shako with green plume above red-and-blue bow-cockade on the front, with brass regimental number above a bugle-horn badge; the jacket was black-braided in hussar style, with pointed cuffs and British-style shoulder-straps. Equipment remained black leather, but small pouches on the front of the waist-belt were adopted; gaiters became pointed-topped. The shako illustrated is after Denis Dighton, showing a black plume, round cockade, bugle-horn over number on the front, and folding, possibly detachable, peak. Dighton shows a plain brown jacket without braid or shoulder-straps but three rows of buttons, plain dark grey gaiter-trousers, and waistbelt with pouch worn at the right of a lion-head clasp, with (apparently) a powder-horn on a shoulder-cord. Armed initially with muskets and short swords, the Caçadores later adopted rifles and sword-bayonets.

Facing-colours for the twelve regiments after 1810–11 were: collars sky-blue for the 4th, 8th and 11th, scarlet for the 5th, 9th and 12th, yellow for the 6th and 10th, and black for the remainder; cuffs sky-blue for the 1st, 4th and 12th, scarlet for the 2nd, 5th and 11th, yellow for the 6th and 7th, and black for the remainder.

26 PORTUGAL:
a) **Gunner, 3rd Foot Artillery, 1808.**
b) **Gunner, 2nd Foot Artillery, 1812.**
c) **Officer, 5th Caçadores, 1812.**

The Caçadores officer wears an 1810–11 shako of more usual style than that illustrated in Plate 25. Rank-distinctions on the 1808 uniform were similar to those illustrated, with lace on the breast, collar and cuffs, gold for field officers and yellow silk for junior ranks.

The Portuguese artillery consisted of four regiments, 1st (Corte), 2nd (Algarve), 3rd (Estremos) and 4th (Oporto); field artillery was of good quality and the personnel well-trained. Garrison artillery was different; many of the guns were antique, some even pressed into service with the allied siege-train (Culzean Castle has a mortar cast in 1716 but used at Badajos in 1812!), and often under-manned: at Almeida two officers, two N.C.O.s and thirty-three men were supposed to man 119 guns! Initially the artillery wore infantry-style uniform with 'barretina' shako, with black plume and red-and-blue cords; later the 'stovepipe' and a uniform with black facings and worsted shoulder-rolls were adopted, the shako with infantry-style plate bearing the regimental number. Ribeiro shows an artillery driver wearing an artillery jacket with brass shoulder-scales, buff breeches, long boots, and bell-topped shako (perhaps captured French?) with small, circular brass plate, cockade, black plume and yellow lace upper band.

Engineer officers wore infantry-style uniform with hats like the staff, with white-tipped black plume, dark blue coatee with black facings and gold lace. One complaint was that there were too many senior officers in the Engineers (two colonels, three captains and only one subaltern at Almeida), who were reluctant to superintend field-works because of their senior rank!

The army's pontoon-train was crewed by landing-parties from British warships, and in 1813 Wellington sanctioned the use of Portuguese seamen and naval officers; they were to receive 'four pairs of shoes in the year; two jackets, two pairs of trousers, and one great coat in the year'.

27 SPAIN:
Aides-de-Camp, 1813.

The uniforms illustrated are typical of the opulent dress affected by Spanish officers. Both come from 1813 portraits by Denis Dighton, of Don Juan Espinosa, A.D.C. to General La Peña (in hussar-style uniform), and Lt-Col. Lardizabel, A.D.C. to General Ballasteros. Both uniforms are 'personal' variations on the regulation blue staff uniform with gold-laced red facings. A Spanish cavalry general painted by Dighton in 1815 – perhaps from sketches made during the war – wears a silver-braided dolman with buff facings beneath a dark blue overcoat with gilt buttons, with a crimson sash with gold barrels and cords, buff breeches, long boots with tops shaped like 'Hessians', and an immense bicorn with circular red-and-blue cockade, gold loop and tassels and red-over-white falling plume, and a plain blue, pointed-ended shabraque.

The British mistrust and derision of

the inefficient and sycophantic Spanish staff centred on the aged Captain-General of Estremadura, Don Gregorio de la Cuesta, an immobile version of Don Quixote (he travelled in a lumbering coach and sat on a horse with the aid of a servant on either side). Despite a bemedalled and lace-covered uniform, his appearance provoked harsh judgements: '... obstinate surly old ignorant fellow ... so violent and obstinate that everybody feared him but his enemies' (Warre); 'perverse, stupid old blockhead' (Colborne); 'that deformed-looking lump of pride, ignorance and treachery' (Costello). Even the Spanish folk-hero the Marqués de la Romana was described by *Times* correspondent Henry Crabb Robinson as looking more 'like a Spanish barber' than a general!

28 SPAIN:
  a) **Officer, Life Guards, 1808.**
  b) **Officer, Regt de la Reyna, 1808.**
  c) **Trooper, Voluntarios de España, 1808.**

The four Life Guard companies wore cavalry uniform, with 'Swedish' cuffs, the coloured squares on the pouch-belt distinguishing companies: Compania Española red, America purple, Italiana dark green, Flamenca yellow. Other ranks wore white lace; turnback-badges consisted of a rampant lion on the outer turnback and a tower on the inner, in white (silver for officers). The infantry equivalent, the 'Albarderos' (halberdiers), wore a similar uniform of infantry cut with lace loops on the lapels, three buttons per cuff, purple knee-stockings, black silver-buckled shoes and were armed with sword and halberd.

The twelve line cavalry regiments wore similar uniform, all with red turnbacks, rampant-lion collar-badge, hat-lace and epaulettes in the button colour; facing-colours are listed in the table.

The first four had lace loops on the lapels; pocket-piping was red for all except Infante (white) and Farnesio (yellow). Various sources give slightly different details in some cases. Other ranks wore dark blue shoulder-straps; square shabraques were dark blue with button-coloured lace edging.

The 'Cazadores' (Chasseurs à

Regt	Facings	Piping	Buttons	Remarks
Rey	red	white	yellow	
Reina	sky blue	red	white	
Principe	red	white	white	
Infante	white	yellow	yellow	
Borbon	red	white	white	
Farnesio	red	yellow	white	
Alcantara	red	green	white	green lapels
España	crimson	crimson	white	yellow collar
Algarve	yellow	yellow	white	
Calatrava	sky blue	sky blue	white	red collar
Santiago	crimson	crimson	white	
Montesa	crimson	white	white	

Cheval) wore braided dolmans and hussar breeches, with fur-crested helmet, the Voluntarios de España with sky-blue facings and waistcoats, the Olivenza Regt red. The Almansa and Villaviciosa Dragoons also adopted Cazador-style uniform with shako (see Plate 29).

The Spanish cavalry was of limited value, their most creditable performance in the war being the charge of Regt el Rey at Talavera, including the capture of four guns. Probably for reasons of economy the troopers seem to have worn canvas gaiters shaped like riding-boots, buttoned on the outer edge. Such 'economies' or mis-appropriation of funds resulted in the 15,000 Spanish cavalry having only 9,000 horses; in June 1808 Regt Reina had 202 horses for 667 men, for example! Years of mis-management partly excuses their desperate reputation in action.

29 SPAIN:
a) **Trooper, Villaviciosa Dragoons, 1808.**
b) **Officer, Maria Luisa Hussars, 1808.**
c) **Officer, Numancia Dragoons, 1808.**

The Dragoons wore distinctive yellow uniform with white lace for all regiments, some sources showing piping of the same colour as the facings (regiments with yellow collars had collar-lace of the facing colour). Turnbacks were red for all, though many authorities (probably following an error in the Conde de Clonard's work on the Spanish cavalry) show them as yellow. Facing-colours were: Regt Rey crimson, Reina light red, Almansa sky blue, Pavia red (yellow collar), Villaviciosa green, Sagunta green (yellow collar), Numancia black, Lusitania black (yellow collar). Collar-badges were of crossed sabres and palm-branch, and the four-button cuff-flap feature was common to many Spanish uniforms. Officers had silver lace and epaulettes; troopers had yellow shoulder-straps piped in the facing-colour. Waistcoats and breeches were yellow, perhaps buff-leather; it is not certain that all trumpeters wore reversed colours. Shabraques were yellow with white lace edging, some sources indicating facing-coloured housing. See *Uniforms of the Napoleonic Wars*, Plate 17.

The Villaviciosa and Almansa Dragoons (both serving with La Romana) wore 'Cazadore' uniform and shako from 1807–08, the Almansa with red facings, white shako-cords and red plume. The Villaviciosa uniform illustrated is after Suhr, who shows a variety of regimental uniforms of this style. All wear the shako with oval plate near the top, with red or red-over-black plume (with black waterproof cover), though an officer's busby has red bag and plume (élite company); the dolman is shown either fastened or open to expose the waistcoat (a trumpeter shown with yellow collar and cuffs); officers had silver epaulettes and lace, breeches without the decorative leather reinforcing but with silver 'darts' or trefoils on the thigh, and one has a green sash with red and white striped barrels. The waistcoat, worn alone for barrack dress, had three rows of buttons on the breast and pointed red cuffs; greatcoats were green. Suhr shows officers wearing single-breasted 'surtout' and 'habit-veste' with cut-open lapels, both in regimental colouring, and red-plumed bicorn. The straight-bladed cavalry sabre is shown either with its regulation brown leather scabbard, or (for officers) brass.

The two hussar regiments wore mirliton caps; the Maria Luisa Regt had a scarlet dolman with sky-blue collar and cuffs, sky-blue pelisse with black fur (no fur on officers' collars), sky-blue breeches, black mirliton with scarlet wing edged white, red plume, and crossed sabres and palm motif on the collar. Regt España had emerald-green dolman with sky-blue collar and cuffs, sky-blue pelisse with black fur and emerald-green collar and cuffs, sky-blue breeches, and mirliton as before with sky-blue wing. Braid was white for both (silver for officers). The Cazadores of the Generalissimo's Guard wore Cazadore shako with white plate, lace and cords, light blue plume, dark blue dolman with red cuffs, white braid, light blue and white barrelled sash, dark blue hussar breeches with white lace, hussar boots and buff gloves.

30 SPAIN:
  a) **Officer, Regt El Rey, 1808.**
  b) **Trooper, Regt Algarve, undress, 1807.**

Both uniforms after Suhr. The officer probably wears 'walking-out' dress, including coatee with closed lapels. Suhr shows this uniform either without sword, or the scabbard carried in the hand with waist-belt wrapped around it, the sabre a thinner-bladed, more ornate version of the usual heavy sabre. For 'undress' Suhr shows single-breasted, unlaced 'surtouts' in regimental colouring. Not all Suhr's pictures conform to regulations; for example, Regt Infante is shown with red facings, perhaps the result of shortages of regulation uniform whilst serving with La Romana's division. Suhr shows extensive use of the coatee with closed lapels, and the enormous proportions of the bicorn worn by officers at various angles from 'fore-and-aft' to 'athwart'. Cigars and umbrellas frequently figure in his sketches.

The trooper wears regulation cavalry fatigue or undress uniform and rides a donkey or mule, perhaps due to shortage of horses. Similar pictures show the sabre worn from a waistbelt and long boots with this uniform. The mitre-shaped fatigue-cap could be worn upside-down, the padded cloth crown turned inside-out, the high front acting as a peak.

31 SPAIN:
  a) **Drum-Major, Regt Princesa, 1808.**
  b) **Musician, Regt Princesa, 1808.**
  c) **Officer, Regt Irlanda, 1808.**

The Spanish army's three Irish regiments were composed of Irish *émigrés* and second- and third-generation Irish of Spanish birth; in addition many Spanish officers bore names like Blake, O'Donnell, O'Neill, O'Daly, O'Donahue, Lacy, Mahony and Sarsfield, generally the most reliable of the army. The Irish regiments wore sky-blue infantry uniform (illustration after Goddard & Booth, who probably incorrectly show collar-badges on the original), Regt Irlanda having yellow facings and buttons, Regt Hibernia the same with sky-blue collar and white collar, and Regt Ultonia with sky-blue lapels edged yellow, yellow cuffs and lapels, and white buttons. The six Swiss regiments of the Spanish army (Wimpfen, Reding Sen., Reding Jun., Beschard, Traxler and Preux) wore similar uniform of dark blue with red collar, lapels, round cuffs, turnbacks and shoulder-straps all edged white, white buttons, red pocket-piping, white waistcoat and breeches, and the bicorn with red cockade edged white with white loop (Preux with blue collar, waistcoat and breeches). One further foreign regiment, Naples, had yellow facings and white buttons, and the single foreign guard unit, the Walloon Guards, had regulation dark blue Guard uniform with red facings, dark blue collar, and white lace.

Spanish musicians wore exotic costume, as shown by the drum-major and child-musician of the Princesa Regt, both after Suhr; neither resemble ordinary regimental uniform. The very wide baldric was a feature of all drum-majors' costume. Suhr shows a cymbal-player of the Princesa in the same hussar dress as the child, the latter employed as fifers and 'mascots', often the sons of regimental musicians. Suhr shows the Zamora Regt's drum-major wearing the same pattern as that illustrated, but black with red facings, no cuff-flaps, and silver lace, the sleeve-seams laced with three inverted 'V's immediately above each cuff, red sash with ornate silver floral embroidery, hat with red, yellow and white plumes, and Hessian boots; Zamora musicians wore the same pattern of coatee of red with black facings, with white lace and hat-plume.

32 SPAIN:
a) **Grenadier, Regt Zamora, 1808.**
b) **Fusilier, Regt de Aragon, 1808.**
c) **Pioneer, Regt Princesa, 1808.**

The thirty-five line regiments had an establishment of seventy officers and 2,186 men each, composed of three battalions of four companies each; in practice the figure was much less, half down to 1,200 and eleven less than 1,000. They wore 1805-pattern white uniform, grenadiers distinguished by tall, plate-less fur caps with large, embroidered hanging bag and cuff-lace as illustrated. Centre companies wore red-plumed bicorns; the four-button cuff-flap is not shown in all contemporary illustrations. Officers had longer coat-tails, epaulettes of the button-colour, scarlet sashes with metallic tassels, and gorgets; sergeants' worsted epaulettes were red or sometimes apparently of the facing-colour. Turnbacks were edged in the facing-colour and bore either a heart- or diamond-badge (both shown by contemporary sources) or grenade-badges for some grenadiers. All regiments carried standard equipment, grenadiers having short sabres with red knot and brass match-case on the shoulder-belt (see Black-and-White Plate 'B'), and brass grenade-badge on the cartridge-box. White breeches and black gaiters were often replaced on campaign by loose trousers, often brown or (as shown by Suhr) checked material. Many contemporary pictures show variations on the standard uniform.

Facing-colours were borne on the collar, lapels, cuffs and flaps and piping; 'W' or 'Y' below indicates white or yellow buttons: Regts Rey (Y), Reina (W), Principe (Y), Soria (W) and Princesa (W) purple facings; Savoia (Y), Corona (W), Africa (Y), Zamora (W) and Sevilla (W) black; Cordoba (Y), Guadalajara (W), Mallorca (Y), Leon (W) and Aragon (W) red; Granada (Y), Valencia (W), Toledo (Y), Murcia (W) and Cantabria (W) sky-blue; Zaragoza (Y), España (W), Burgos (Y), Asturias (W) and Fijo de Ceuta (W) green; Navara (Y), America (W), Malaga (Y), Jaen (W) and Ordenes Militares (W) dark blue; Estramadura (Y), Voluntarios de Castilla (W), Voluntarios de la Corona (Y), Voluntarios del Estado (W) and Borbon (W) crimson. White lapels worn by Regts Princesa, Sevilla, Aragon, Cantabria, Fijo de Ceuta, Ordenes Militares and Borbon; white collars by Regts Principe, Soria, Africa, Zamora, Mallorca, Leon, Toledo, Murcia, Burgos, Asturias, Malaga, Jaen, Voluntarios de la Corona and Voluntarios del Estado. Among minor differences shown by some contemporary sources are the Zamora's brown collars, shown by Suhr.

Pioneers' ornate uniforms usually included fur cap with elaborate plate, often grenadier uniform, and apron with small pockets with draw-string tops to hold nails. The Princesa pioneer illustrated (after Suhr) wears what may be the 1802 blue uniform, officially replaced in 1805 but continuing in some cases until worn-out.

33 SPAIN:
a) **Officer, 2nd Catalonian Light Infantry, 1808.**
b) **Private, 2nd Catalonian Light Infantry, 1808.**
c) **Sergeant, Cazadores, Light Infantry, 1813.**

Each of the twelve light infantry battalions in 1808 comprised six companies. The hussar uniform introduced in 1802 was replaced in 1805–6, but Suhr shows its use long after official replacement. The officer wears the dolman open to expose the waistcoat, and bicorn with oddly-shaped loop. Other ranks' dolmans had yellow lace and red shoulder-straps piped yellow; they wore white knee-breeches and stockings (shown light brown by Knötel, after Suhr, with peasant sandals), the typically-Spanish pouch made up of cartridge-tubes at the front of the waist, and scarlet girdle. The head-dress was a black, fur-crested 'round hat' similar in appearance to the British 'Tarleton', with a peak/brim of black leather edged brass, brass band around the bottom, small oval brass plate on the front of the fur crest, and green plume rising from bow-cockade on the left. For all ranks the dolman was laced hussar-fashion on the rear seams.

The dark blue 1806 uniform was of line infantry style, with green-plumed bicorn. Facing-colours on cuffs, cuff-flaps, turnbacks, lapels, collar and piping were: 1st and 2nd Aragon and Barbastro red; 1st and 2nd Catalonian, Tarragona, Gerona, 1st and 2nd Barcelona yellow; Voluntarios de Valencia, Voluntarios de Navarra, and Campomayor crimson. Blue lapels for Tarragona, 1st Barcelona, Barbastro and

Voluntarios de Navarra; blue collar for 2nd Catalonian, 2nd Aragon, 2nd Barcelona and Campomayor; blue piping for 2nd Aragon, Barbastro, Campomayor, Voluntarios de Valencia and Navarra. Yellow buttons for both Catalonian and Tarragona Regts, and white for the remainder.

The 1812 'British' uniform was like that of the line (Plates 35–36) with similar company distinctions, but entirely light blue (some sources show dark blue). In undress uniform, all Spanish infantry other ranks wore the sleeved waistcoat, with regimentally-coloured forage-cap, usually of the shape illustrated (after Suhr). White undress jackets with regimental facings and small shoulder-straps were also worn, over the shirt and sometimes the waistcoat; breeches and stockings were worn with this uniform, with sandals or short gaiters and boots. Design of undress uniform varied between regiments.

34 SPAIN:
a) Officer, Artillery, 1808.
b) Private, Regt Muerte, 1808.

Despite years of neglect, the artillery was among the best of the Spanish army. Thirty-four foot, six horse and twenty-one garrison batteries mustered about 240 guns (many below the establishment of six guns each); for the four horse and thirty-two field batteries left after the departure of La Romana's division there were only 400 draught horses for 216 guns, limbers and caissons. Hence the guns had to be dragged by mules, rendering them slow and incapable of manoeuvre in action. Gunners rarely abandoned their pieces, suffering huge losses when over-run, every defeat thus resulting in the loss of large numbers of cannon and trained personnel.

The officer illustrated (after Suhr) wears dark blue artillery uniform with red facings and grenade insignia. A horse artilleryman sketched at the same time wears similar hat and coatee, but dark blue trousers and carries a brass-sheathed light cavalry sabre on a shoulder-belt. Goddard & Booth show a similar gunner's uniform (Black-and-White Plate 'B') with a 'round hat' with the brim fastened up at the front, with lace loop and plume, white overalls and red waistcoat; an officer has similar uniform, with hat-brim turned up on the left side, white breeches and black knee-gaiters – unusual as the hat was a distinction of Guard artillery.

Early in the war, unco-ordinated regional 'juntas' raised a huge number of small units, either based on extant militia, formed from remnants of regular corps, or from volunteers. Scores of unlikely costumes were in evidence, though many had only semi-civilian dress. The 'Muerte' ('Death') Regt illustrated is typical, the skull and crossed bones device a common feature on volunteer uniforms. Other 'junta' forces are illustrated in Black-and-White Plates 'C' and 'D'; many, however, dressed in brown local cloth jackets and knee breeches, with peasant footwear. The Regt Victoria, for example, had tail-less brown jackets with red collar, cuffs and lapels, brown breeches, and black 'round hat' with a brass oval plate on the front, and red cockade.

The official embodied militia in 1808 consisted of forty-three battalions totalling some 30,000 men, named from towns in whose district they were raised – Alcazar, Badajos, Lugo, etc. With officers drawn from local landowners, the militia was seemingly almost as efficient as the regulars. Militia uniforms were of line pattern, white with red facings, white waistcoat and breeches; yellow metal buttons, red turnbacks bearing gold fleur-de-lys badges (officers) or white triangles (other ranks). Four regiments – Old Castile, New Castile, Andalusia and Galicia – were grenadiers, with a strength of between 1,300 to 1,600.

35 SPAIN:
a) Fusilier Officer, Infantry, 1812.
b) Grenadier, Infantry, 1812.

From about 1812, many Spanish infantry units received the so-called 'British' uniform, consisting of 'stovepipe' cap, single-breasted dark blue jacket with red facings, and overalls. Based on British patterns, some items were manufactured in Britain (as were many Portuguese), surpluses eventually being sold to Prussia (see *Uniforms of Waterloo*, Plate 71). Overalls (officially light blue) were often grey or made from brown local cloth. Whilst not universal, the 'British' uniform was worn, for example, by the Morillo Division in the Vittoria and Pyrenees campaigns.

Grenadiers had red shako-plume and lace, and brass grenade plate; the 'lace' on the shako was decorative around the bottom, but probably served as a chin-strap when not tied up in a bow on top of the cap. Grenadiers had padded blue wings with red fringes, and grenadier sergeants red fringed epaulettes. 'Cazadores' (light company) had green plume and shako-lace, white metal or brass hunting-horn plate and green wing-fringes; sergeants green epaulettes. Fusiliers (centre companies) had white plume and shako-lace, brass rampant lion shako-plate, and three-pointed dark blue shoulder-straps with red piping; sergeants white epaulettes. Officers' uniforms had longer coat-tails, gold epaulettes, gilt buttons, red or red-and-gold sash, gilt shako-plates and (possibly) gold shako-lace. Several sources show small collar-badges for all ranks, but there is insufficient evidence to prove whether this was a rampant-lion design or the initial letter of the regiment, shown in this case as 'L' for 'Leon', a distinguished part of Morillo's Division which served at Roncevalles. Equipment was often British-pattern, though not all sources show the oval shoulder-belt plate, perhaps restricted to grenadiers; canteens varied, often barrel-shaped. Officers had black leather sword-belts; the man illustrated has breeches of 'local' cloth and wears the Spanish Royal arms on the gorget.

36 SPAIN:
a) Private, Infantry, 1812.
b) Cazadore Officer, Infantry, 1812.
c) Officer, Infantry, 1812.

Plate 36 continues to illustrate the 'British' uniform. The Cazadore officer has light company distinctions of plume, shako-lace and plate. The Fusilier officer is taken from an eye-witness sketch from the 'Frankfurt Collection', retaining the bicorn with fusilier plume. The tattered uniform reflects the usual state of 'campaign dress', though the subject of the original had managed to retain his fashionable yellow gloves! He wears a straight-bladed sword from a 'frog', though many (not just flank company officers) preferred the curved sabre worn on slings.

The greatcoated figure is from St Clair, showing typical 'foul weather' costume including waterproof shako-cover and mittens. Arms included a large quantity of British muskets, or Spanish-manufactured firearms characterized by the straight, rather than curved, hammer.

37 SPAIN:
a) Private, Medina Sidonia Regt, 1813.
b) Officer, Cortes Regt, 1813.

In the later stages of the war some Spanish units adopted bell-topped shakos and a variety of uniform-colours and patterns. The two illustrated are taken from Denis Dighton watercolours of 1813. The Medina Sidonia Regt bore the Royal cypher 'F VII' on the shako, large cockades being typical of this type of uniform. The collar bears the regimental initials, MS, proving that this style of badge was in use (see Plate 35), and the belt-plate the popular skull-and-crossed-bones. The Cortes Regt officer wears the old-pattern bicorn and a gold-embroidered coatee. Surtees comments on the dress of Spanish officers seen in Cadiz (1811): 'It was really absurd and ludicrous to see the strange figures they generally made themselves. In one regiment alone you might have observed more different uniforms than both we and the French have in all our armies. One would have ... a blue coat turned up with red, with a chaco [*sic*] and a straight sword, the uniform prescribed for officers of the infantry ... the next would have ... a hussar dress, with an enormous sabre dangling by his side; another would have had a red coat, a fourth yellow, a fifth white, and so on. In short, all the colours of the rainbow were generally exhibited in the uniforms of one regiment's officers; and every one of them appeared to vie with the other who could make the greatest harlequin of himself ...'

A typical list of Spanish uniforms is provided in the orders of Lt-Gen. Maitland when Whittingham's Spanish Division joined the army for service in eastern Spain in 1812: Majorca Grenadiers, blue jackets faced sky-blue, buff 'cape' (collar) and cap (?), red plume, blue pantaloons and buff leather equipment; Murcia Grenadiers, blue jackets faced yellow, sky-blue breeches, black leather equipment; 2nd Majorca Regt, blue jackets faced red, blue pantaloons and blue (?) leather equipment; Majorca Cazadores, uniformed like the British 95th; Battalion of Light Companies, as their respective regiments, plus two companies of Cordova Regt wearing blue jackets with crimson facings (i.e. lapels), buff collar and cuffs; 'Grenadier Companies of Guadalajara', blue jackets faced buff, buff leather equipment. 'All the regiments have also buff pantaloons, and their caps are broader above than below.' There were in addition the Almansa Hussars, dressed like the British 10th Hussars; Olivenza Dragoons, yellow jackets faced red, helmet like the 'Tarleton' with red plume; Artillery, blue jackets faced red, infantry shako with red plume; Artificers, blue jackets faced red, red plume, and leather apron. Regimental titles above may be a little confused as the Division is usually listed as containing the Burgos Regt and Cuesta Grenadiers instead of the 2nd Majorca and Majorca Grenadiers.

38 SPAIN:
a) Private, Walloon Guards, 1813.
b) Field Officer, Toledo Regt, 1813.

Two further uniforms from Dighton, the officer from a portrait of Col. Don Juan de Gonzales, 'a sketch from life at Cadiz', dated 22 June 1813. The Toledo Regt private shown by Dighton wears brown infantry uniform with yellow collar, round cuffs, lapels and tufted shoulder-straps, white metal buttons, long white pantaloons, black ankle-gaiters and leather equipment.

The Walloon Guards private wears a variation on the old dark blue Guard uniform with red facings and white lace, with bell-topped shako bearing brass plate; the long gaiters are another relic of the old dress. The use of bell-topped shakos by the Spanish was quite widespread, 'TS' of the British 71st noting how in the Pyrenees the British mistook a French column for Spaniards, the French greatcoats and 'white covers on their hats, exactly resembling the Spanish', as did Surtees at Vittoria: 'They were dressed in blue, and had caps covered with white canvass [*sic*]. I took them for Spaniards ...' Not all Spanish infantry wore the shako, Dighton painting an officer of the 'Loyal Distinguished Cadiz Volunteers' in 1813 wearing a black 'round hat' with white metal plate and white plume on the left, brown uniform with russet facings, silver lace and epaulette on the right shoulder, white waistcoat, yellow breeches, silver-laced black 'Hessian' boots and an oval silver badge on the right forearm.

Shown in this plate is the uniquely-Spanish cartridge-tube assembly, worn at the front of the waistbelt (often with a flap to cover the top), and the Spanish-manufactured musket with straight hammer.

39 SPAIN:
a) Guerrilla officer, 1813.
b) Guerrilla.
c) Catalonian volunteer.

Guerrilla activity – the most gruesome feature of the Peninsular War – was often a spontaneous outburst by peasants armed with knives and agricultural tools; organized raids by local landowners developed into a no-quarter war of immense proportion, involving permanent bands often several hundred strong. Atrocities were perpetrated by both sides as the French answered Spanish butchery by reprisal. Wellington wrote that 'The Spanish people are like gunpowder – the least spark inflames them ... there is no violence or outrage they do not commit ... the Spaniard is an undisciplined savage who obeys no law ... ready with his knife or firelock to commit murder ...'

The best-organized bands were led by folk-hero bandit-chiefs: Martin Diaz, alias El Empecinado (Inky Face), a labourer's son; Mina, a student; Don Julian Sanchez, who decapitated French couriers and sent their despatches to Wellington. In December

1808 the Central Junta tried to regularize 'partidas' (guerrilla bands) to a strength of 100 infantry or 50 cavalry; but Espoz y Mina (Mina's uncle) could field 8,000 men and defeated the French in open battle. Though the guerrillas largely depended upon British assistance, Wellington's task would have been immeasurably harder without them, as the French had constantly to fight on two fronts. Inevitably, much genuine banditry was disguised as patriotism, for example the infamous 'Marshal Stockport', a renegade French sergeant who led a band of 300 French, British and Portuguese deserters in a career of brutality until captured and shot by the French.

Very few guerrillas had recognizable 'uniform' though many wore items of uniform or quasi-military dress. The officer illustrated is from a Dighton picture of Jose de Espin, 'one of Don Juan Martin's Chiefs', wearing a personally-designed uniform including large hat-cockade and skull-and-crossed bones insignia. Other Dighton pictures showing guerrillas in 'uniform' (see Black-and-White Plate 'D') may not be accurate; for example, 'Don Youlen's Corps' are shown in hussar dress, blue faced scarlet with yellow braid, red-striped blue overalls with black leather reinforcing, white belts and brown busby with red bag. A more typical dress shown by Dighton illustrates a patch-eyed officer in huge black bicorn, dark green single-breasted frock-coat with silver buttons, brown overalls with black leather reinforcing, and gilt-mounted light cavalry sabre.

The Catalonian volunteer wears semi-military dress made from civilian cloth, as described by Col. F. P. Robinson in 1812: 'sheep ... are a very dark brown ... which saves the trouble of dying the cloth ... Peasants clothed in a brown short Jacket, waistcoat – breeches Leggins [sic] and Cloak ...' Contemporary pictures show extensive use of sandals or soft leather boots with turned-over tops, a wide variety of 'round hats', sombreros and cloth stocking-caps, hair tied in a scarf or hair-net, and captured or looted military items. Gleig describes a troop 'arrayed in green jackets with slouched hats and long feathers, others in blue, helmeted like our yeomanry or artillery drivers, while not a few wore cuirasses and brazen headpieces such as they had probably plundered from their slaughtered enemies'. Weapons consisted of any captured sabre or musket, pistols worn in holsters or tucked into the waist-belt or girdle, farm tools, machetes, lances and crudely-made pikes; the blunderbuss was a favourite weapon, firing a variety of shot, Marbot being hit by a flat lead bullet the size of a half-crown with a notched edge, guaranteed to cause fearful injury. See also *Uniforms of the Napoleonic Wars*, Plate 24.

40 FRANCE:
a) **Aide-de-Camp, 1813.**
b) **General Lefebvre-Desnoëttes, 1808.**

General Lefebvre-Desnoëttes was appointed Colonel-Major of the Imperial Guard Chasseurs à Cheval in January 1808. Serving with his regiment at Benevente in December 1808, he was wounded and captured by Private Levi Grisdall of the British 10th Hussars. He escaped to France from captivity in

Britain by breaking his parole in May 1812. He is illustrated in regimental uniform, after William Heath, the pelisse worn as a jacket, obscuring the gold-laced green dolman with scarlet facings. Both dolman and pelisse had eight lines of lace around the cuff, apparently a distinction reserved for general officers of the Guard when in regimental uniform. The busby-cockade bore a gold-embroidered Imperial eagle and the 'raquettes' three silver stars indicative of rank; the green portion of plume is unusual. Decorations were those of Commandant of the Légion d'Honneur and the breast-star of the Order of Fidelity of Baden, a red-enamelled four-armed cross with gilt devices, on a silver star. The regimental sabretache bore a gold eagle on ermine backing, on a green ground, edged with gold lace, though a sabretache ascribed to Lefebvre-Desnoëttes lacks the heavy gold fringe shown by other sources. For Staff uniform, see *Uniforms of the Napoleonic Wars*, Plates 8/9 and 71, and *Uniforms of the Retreat from Moscow*, Plates 1 and 48. For Chasseurs' uniform, see *Uniforms of Waterloo*, Plate 48, *Uniforms of the Napoleonic Wars*, Plate 27, and *Uniforms of the Retreat from Moscow*, Plate 4. Surtees records their dress at Benevente as 'dark-green long coats, with high bearskin-caps', suggesting use of the coatee rather than the hussar uniform.

French Aides-de-Camp wore varied costume, either staff uniform, regimental uniform with 'staff' distinctions, or patterns reserved for the staff of a particular marshal or general. Several versions of the uniform of Soult's aides exist, that illustrated after El Guil, though Boisselier shows black pompom-tuft and belt, red pouch-belt and grey overalls, and another source silver lace and shako-cords and sky-blue pouch-belt. Bucquoy shows a different uniform, based perhaps on that of the 2nd Hussars: sky-blue shako with gold ornaments, dark brown 'habit' with sky-blue piping, silver-braided dark brown waistcoat, silver epaulettes, gold-laced red belts, gold-laced sky-blue hussar breeches, and 'Hessian' boots; the ground-colour of the uniform is also shown as yellow, and another source shows the same breeches, shako with sky-blue cloth cover, and white-furred white pelisse with gold braid. Any of the latter could be 'personalized' uniforms based on regimental dress.

Examples of non-regulation dress worn on campaign are provided by Parquin's description of Divisional Paymaster Malet in August 1811: cornflower-blue jacket with silver embroidery, white cashmere trousers and close-fitting riding-boots (presumably civilian dress), and by Marbot's attempt to conceal a bandage on his head which prevented the wear of either busby or bicorn. Not wishing to appear bareheaded before Napoleon, he made a mameluke-style turban out of a red skull-cap and a silk handkerchief, which was apparently not considered an eccentric addition to his A.D.C. uniform!

41 FRANCE:
    a) **Private, Young Guard, 1810.**
    b) **Private, Chasseurs à Pied, Imperial Guard, 1808.**
    c) **Trumpeter, Marines of the Guard, 1808.**

A variation on the well-known 'Old

Guard' uniform, the Imperial Guard Chasseur à Pied illustrated (after an eye-witness sketch of their short Peninsula service, 1808–09) shows the undress sleeved waistcoat and loose linen overalls worn as a concession to the climate. Unusual features are the epaulettes (usually depicted as green with red crescents until 1808, and red with green strap thereafter), and the coloured bearskin-tassel, usually white. Unlike the Grenadiers', Chasseurs' caps had no plate or rear patch. Equipment included hide knapsack, black leather cartridge-box bearing brass crowned eagle badge (usually covered with white linen bearing a black-painted eagle in the centre and alternate grenades and hunting-horns in the corners, on campaign), the 'sabre-briquet' (short sabre and bayonet in combined frog) and the unofficial canteen or gourd. The sword-knot (when worn) was white with green knot and scarlet tassel, mixed with gold for N.C.O.s, whose epaulettes had gold lace trim. The white cap-cords (red, green and gold for N.C.O.s) were omitted on campaign. See *Uniforms of Waterloo*, Plates 49–50, *Uniforms of the Napoleonic Wars*, Plate 64, and *Uniforms of the Retreat from Moscow*, Plate 2.

The Guard Marines (a battalion of which was captured at Baylen) wore dark blue dolman with orange braid, replaced on campaign by a double-breasted 'caracot' (short jacket). Many contemporary pictures show variations, that illustrated based on a Suhr sketch (1806–07). Musicians' sky-blue uniform (dolmans in full dress) had scarlet-orange lace, with old-pattern shako with detachable peak and mixed scarlet and white cords (other sources show musicians' shako- and trumpet-cords mixed red and yellow); the other ranks' brass shoulder-scales are not shown by Suhr. The distinctive marine-pattern sabre was carried by all ranks, the shoulder-belt plate bearing an embossed anchor. Some sources show the cockade worn on the side of the shako at this period, though Weiland, Suhr, Zimmermann and Henschel all show the frontal cockade for 1806–08. See *Uniforms of Waterloo*, Plate 53.

Several Young Guard regiments saw extensive service in Spain. The figure illustrated (after sketches by El Guil) has a waterproof shako-cover bearing a painted eagle, and unusual brown single-breasted greatcoat with red piping presumably worn over the regulation blue coatee. El Guil shows a variety of legwear – white overalls, loose buff trousers, grey or blue trousers with red stripe; cartridge-boxes are shown with white linen cover bearing yellow-painted eagle. Some troops drafted into the Guard apparently wore their line uniform with guard distinctions tacked on, until an official issue of Guard uniform could be made.

42 FRANCE:
a) Trooper, 3rd Dragoons, 1810.
b) Officer, 20th Dragoons, 1810.

Dragoons (originally mounted infantry) provided the backbone of French anti-guerrilla activity; mobile and well-armed, they served in small detachments, escorting supplies and couriers and protecting lines of communication. Most regiments also served against the Allied field army. Their uniform included brass helmet (hence the Spanish nickname, 'golden heads') with horsehair mane, dark green coat with cut-back lapels, and breeches and boots (full dress). Common variations on campaign included overalls (grey or brown), dark green single-breasted 'surtout', and linen helmet-covers. The 1812-pattern jacket with lapels closed to the waist may have been worn in Spain in 1813-14, but its use was restricted (see *Uniforms of Waterloo*, Plate 55, and *Uniforms of the Retreat from Moscow*, Plate 11). Plumes were omitted on campaign, but varied considerably for full dress, that illustrated after Martinet; variously shown by contemporary sources, they included red over black; green over red (7th, 8th, 12th, 13th), crimson (10th), yellow over white (24th), red (1st, 22nd), white (4th, 5th, 8th, 11th, 16th, 17th, 19th, 21st, 24th), red over white (12th, 18th), facing-colour over green (1st, 2nd, 6th, 19th, 20th, 25th), and white over yellow (20th); how many of these were actually worn is unknown. Élite companies and pioneers often wore bearskin caps, even on campaign; for example, Capt. Gordon of the British 15th Hussars records mistaking a French élite dragoon officer for a member of his own regiment, the Frenchman wearing a cloak and no bearskin-ornaments.

Facing-colours were borne on lapels, turnbacks, collar, cuffs and cuff-flaps of the coatee (the 'surtout' had coloured collar and cuffs or was all-green); facings for regiments serving in the Peninsula were: 1st-6th, scarlet; 8th-12th carmine; 13th-18th rose-pink; 19th-22nd and 24th yellow; 25th-27th orange. Green collars (sometimes piped in the facing-colour) worn by 2nd, 5th, 8th, 11th, 14th, 17th, 20th and 26th; green cuffs by 3rd, 6th, 9th, 12th, 15th, 18th, 24th and 27th; green cuff-flaps by 2nd, 5th, 8th, 11th, 17th, 20th and 26th; pockets vertical for 4th-6th, 10th-12th, 16th-18th, 22nd and 24th, and horizontal for the remainder. Shoulder-straps were green with facing-coloured piping, though some élites had red epaulettes and white epaulettes were probably worn for a time by at least the 2nd, 9th, 17th, 19th and 22nd. Turnback-badges were green grenades (silver for officers); officers had silver epaulettes, Colonel two, Major two with gold straps, 'chef d'escadron' silver epaulette on left and shoulder-strap on right, captain as 'chef d'escadron' but thin fringe on left, lieutenant as captain with a scarlet line on the strap, and 2nd lieutenants two lines. Square-cut shabraques were green with silver lace (officers), and (after 1812) sheepskin with 'wolf-tooth' edging over green shabraques with white lace. Officers' shabraques bore silver grenades in the rear corners and other ranks' a white regimental number, but variations are recorded.

A considerable quantity of brown dragoon uniforms were worn due to shortages of green cloth; though locally-made not all were hastily-produced, most having correct facings and insignia. Breeches and cossack-style trousers were made of the same material, often portrayed as maroon. A common campaign style was to wear the sword-belt extended over the right shoulder, giving the appearance of cross-belts with the carbine- and pouch-belts worn over the left. The 3rd Regt served in Spain from 1808-11 and the 20th from 1808-12.

43 FRANCE:
   a) **Officer, 27th Chasseurs à Cheval, 1809.**
   b) **Trooper, 10th Chasseurs à Cheval, 1810.**

Three styles of Chasseur à Cheval uniform were worn during the Peninsular War, initially the dark green 'habit' with cut-open, pointed-ended lapels with collar, cuffs and piping in the facing-colour (some may still have worn the dolman at the beginning). The 1812 regulations introduced a 'habit' with closed lapels, coloured as before; and the single-breasted 'surtout' with facing-coloured collar, cuffs, turnbacks and piping (as illustrated) was also worn. The green breeches and 'Hessian' boots were replaced on campaign by overalls, usually green with black leather reinforcing. Shakos varied, some with diamond-plate, some with 'tricolor' rosette on the front, with or without white cords. On campaign fabric shako-covers were common, sometimes with a 'tricolor' rosette painted on the front. Full-dress plumes (green with red tip for the 10th) were replaced on service by pompoms, red, sky-blue, orange and violet for the 1st–4th squadrons respectively, often with white inner disc for the 2nd Company of each squadron. Élite companies wore red plume and epaulettes, often retained the busby, and sometimes had red lace chevrons on the shako.

The Chevau-Légers d'Aremberg (a Belgian corps) became the 27th Chasseurs in May 1808. The old name continued for some time, Napoleon writing to Joseph in January 1809: 'The regiment of Aremberg, which is the 27th chasseurs ... consists of 1,000 men and 1,000 horses; it is almost entirely composed of Belgians'. It is uncertain which uniform was worn in the Peninsula, but the 'chef d'escadron' illustrated (after Suhr) shows a hussar uniform in use in 1808, at least for part of the regiment (it has been suggested that hussar uniform was restricted to the Duc d'Aremberg's personal contingent of ninety-nine men and three officers); the green dolman with 'amaranth' facings and yellow lace (gold for officers) is omitted in this case, the pelisse worn over the gold-braided 'amaranth' waistcoat. Apparently various issues of 'surtouts' and 'habits' were made, both long- and short-tailed. The usual chasseur officer's shabraque was pointed-ended; other ranks had white sheepskins with facing-coloured 'wolf-tooth' edging, but variations existed.

Facing-colours for other regiments engaged in the war: 5th yellow; 7th pink; 10th, 11th, 12th crimson; 13th, 14th, 15th orange; 20th, 21st light orange; 24th dark orange; 26th madder red; 28th amaranth. Green collars worn by 5th, 11th, 14th, 20th and 26th; collars of the facing-colour were piped green, and vice-versa. Some musicians (e.g. the 10th's) wore reversed colours but there were many variations. See also *Uniforms of Waterloo*, Plates 56/57, and *Uniforms of the Retreat from Moscow*, Plate 7.

44 FRANCE:
   a) **Trooper, Élite Company, 4th Hussars, 1808.**
   b) **Officer, 2nd Hussars, 1811.**

French hussar costume included the typical dolman, pelisse, barrelled sash and (for many officers and élite companies) fur busby, other companies wearing the shako in various colours, with either diamond- or eagle-plate or lace rosette, often with red lace chevrons for élites; the cylindrical shako was adopted in 1813-14. The trooper illustrated wears the pelisse as a jacket, service overalls instead of the full dress breeches and 'Hessian' boots, and the greatcoat as a shoulder-roll, but retains the busby-ornaments (often removed on campaign) and laced full dress sabretache instead of the plain black version with brass badge or numeral. The red plume indicates élite status (1st Company, 1st Squadron), others wearing the shako (red cloth after 1807 with brass diamond-plate for the 4th), with a plume either black or yellow with black base (Martinet, 1807). Company pompoms were like those of the Chasseurs à Cheval (Plate 43). The 4th's élites had an unusual brass grenade badge on the busby, mentioned in a letter of September 1811 by Col. Christophe, who also noted that his élites rode black horses and had black sheepskins at that date. Officers had dark blue cloth pointed-ended shabraques with gold lace edging and scarlet piping on the outer edge.

The 2nd Hussars officer (partly based on a portrait of Lieut. de Rocca) wears loose overalls and the light blue shako with silver lace and rosette enclosed in a cover. Other regimental details shown by various sources for 1811 include sky-blue or chocolate-brown breeches with 'Hessian' boots, short black gauntlets for officers, black shakos for other ranks, and black busbies with scarlet plume and sky-blue bag for élites.

Uniform-details for units serving in Spain:

Regt	Dolman	Collar	Cuffs	Pelisse	Breeches	Lace	Plume
1	sky-blue	sky-blue	red	sky-blue	sky-blue	white	black
2	brown	brown	sky-blue	brown	sky-blue	white	black
3	grey	grey	red	grey	grey	red	black
4	blue	blue	red	red	blue	yellow	black
5	sky-blue	sky-blue	white	white	sky-blue	yellow	white
10	sky-blue	red	red	sky-blue	sky-blue	white	black, red base

Officers' lace was silver or gold accordingly; pelisse-fur black and lining white. Barrelled sashes were red and yellow for 4th and 5th, and red and white for the remainder. The 3rd had white buttons, silver officers' lace and red shako-cords. Officers' shabraques were usually of the dolman-colour with metallic lace edging; other ranks' sheepskins usually with red 'wolf-tooth' edging (2nd and 5th sky-blue). Contemporary examples of trumpeters' multi-coloured costume: 1st red dolman with blue cuffs, red pelisse; 2nd light blue dolman with brown cuffs, light blue pelisse; 3rd red dolman with grey cuffs, red pelisse; 4th red dolman with blue cuffs, blue pelisse; 5th white dolman with sky-blue cuffs, blue pelisse; 10th red dolman with blue collar and cuffs. See also *Uniforms of the Napoleonic Wars*, Plate 7, *Uniforms of Waterloo*, Plate

59, and *Uniforms of the Retreat from Moscow*, Plate 8.

45 FRANCE:
a) Trooper, 13th Cuirassiers, 1810.
b) Maréchal-des-Logis, 1st Lancers, Vistula Legion.

Originally the 'Légion Polacco-Italienne' of the Westphalian Army, the Polish Vistula Legion transferred to French service in March 1808 with an establishment of three infantry and one lancer regiments, increased by one regiment of each in 1810. Detached in June 1811, the lancers became the 7th and 8th Chevau-Léger-Lanciers; after distinguished service in Spain and Russia, the depleted infantry units were amalgamated in June 1813 into the Vistula Regiment, disbanded 1814. The lancers' most famous action was Albuera, their charge wrecking Colborne's British brigade; the infantry won great distinction at Saragossa (1808-9) losing a third of their strength in street-fighting, thereafter operating with Suchet.

The Lancers wore the Polish 'kurtka' jacket with reversible lapels, forming a yellow plastron in full dress, and rear seams piped yellow; the czapka bore the Polish Maltese cross badge upon the cockade, but initially no plate, though some sources show the conventional 'sunburst' design, with blue cloth top, white cords and piping. The élite company had a white plume in full dress, others being shown with black, white-over-black or blue-over-black plumes. The aiguillette was worn by the élite company (silver, on the right shoulder for officers) and a white (or silver) epaulette on the opposite shoulder; other companies had blue shoulder-straps piped yellow. N.C.O. rank-markings were: 'Brigadier' one silver chevron above cuff; 'Fourrier' the same with a diagonal silver stripe on the upper arm and two silver lines on the epaulette-strap; 'Marécal-des-Logis' two silver chevrons, epaulette as 'Fourrier'; 'Marécal-des-Logis-Chef' as before but three chevrons. Lance-pennons were crimson-over-white or vice-versa. shabraques were cream sheepskin with yellow 'wolf-tooth' edging or pointed-ended dark blue cloth with silver lace for officers (this pattern with yellow lace edging shown by some sources for troopers). In August 1810 the 106-strong élite company was appointed Suchet's escort; they apparently carried the regimental guidon, an old banner of the Polish Legion. The Vistula infantry wore blue French-style uniform with yellow facings; see *Uniforms of the Napoleonic Wars*, Plate 48, and *Uniforms of the Retreat from Moscow*, Plates 9 and 25.

The only cuirassier regiment to serve in the Peninsula, the 13th was formed in 1808 from the 1st Provisional Heavy Cavalry which incorporated elements of the 1st, 2nd and 3rd Cuirassiers and 1st and 2nd Carabiniers. The 13th's uniform was of regulation style but after c. 1809 apparently of brown Spanish cloth, there being insufficient dark blue. Their maroon facings were known as '*lie-de-vin*' – 'wine dregs'. In addition to breeches and boots, probably brown baggy overalls (perhaps piped red) were used. The red plume was removed on service and the helmet's horsehair mane often braided and tied on one side; not until 1813 was the regimental number borne on the helmets. Officers had silver buttons and epaulettes; the dark blue shabraques were square-cut, with white lace edging. Trumpeters wore 'reversed colours' with white epaulettes, helmet-mane, aigrette and perhaps loops on their dark blue lapels; they did not wear the cuirass. See *Uniforms of the Napoleonic Wars*, Plate 11, *Uniforms of Waterloo*, Plate 54, and *Uniforms of the Retreat from Moscow*, Plate 6.

46 FRANCE:
  a) **Fusilier, Infantry, 1813.**
  b) **Grenadier, Infantry, 1809.**
  c) **Grenadier, 14th Line, 1808.**

French infantry battalions consisted of seven fusilier (centre) and one grenadier companies until 1807, when the fusiliers were reduced to four and a voltigeur company added. A white uniform was authorized in 1806 but its actual issue was very limited; tradition asserts that the sight of bloodstained white uniforms at Eylau (1807) caused Napoleon to revert to blue in June 1807, but probably some white dress was worn in the opening stage of the Peninsular War, the blue not being re-issued in time. Facing-colours of regiments which *could* have worn white in the Peninsula are shown below.

White items were piped in the facing-colour; voltigeurs usually wore yellow collars (piped in the facing for 14th and

Regt	Collar	Cuffs	Flaps	Lapels	Pockets	Buttons
8th	green	green	green	white	vertical	white
14th	white	black	white	black	vertical	white
15th	black	white	white	black	vertical	white
16th	black	black	—	white	vertical	white
24th	scarlet	scarlet	scarlet	white	vertical	white
28th	brown	brown	brown	white	horizontal	yellow
34th	white	violet	white	violet	horizontal	yellow
86th	white	lt green	white	lt green	vertical	white

86th). Some sources show different details, Suhr for example showing white cuffs piped black for the 14th, perhaps a distinction between battalions. Turnbacks were of the facing-colour.

The dark blue coatee with white lapels and red facings was replaced in January 1812 by the short-tailed 'habit-veste' with closed lapels, its actual introduction often delayed until 1814. The 1812 shako bore eagle-on-shield plate and no cords, though the old diamond-plate and regimental variations often continued in use. Company distinctions remained constant: grenadiers, red plumes, epaulette, grenade turnback-badges and sometimes shako-lace and cords; voltigeurs, combinations of green and/or yellow and red plumes, epaulettes, hunting-horn turnback-badges, shako-cords and lace and often yellow collars; fusiliers, blue shoulder-straps, often blue crowned 'N' turnback-badges, and padded cloth discs above the shako-cockade, green for the 1st company, 2nd sky-blue, 3rd orange and 4th violet, often solid-coloured for 1st battalions and with white centre for the regiment's remaining battalions. There were many regimental variations: see *Uniforms of the Napoleonic Wars*, Plate 14, *Uniforms of Waterloo*, Plates 61 and 62, and *Uniforms of the Retreat from Moscow*, Plates 12, 13 and 16.

Legwear varied from white breeches and black gaiters to loose trousers for campaign, of white or unbleached linen or brown Spanish cloth. Equipment consisted of hide knapsack, cartridge-box often bearing company badges (i.e. grenade or hunting-horn), and for élites and fusilier N.C.O.s the 'sabre-briquet' sabre-and-bayonet assemblage (red sword-knots for grenadiers and yellow, green and/or red for voltigeurs). Those not armed with the sabre had but one shoulder-belt, with the bayonet-scabbard worn on the front. Among unofficial impedimenta always carried was a water-canteen or gourd, of which there was no official issue. The grenadier in greatcoat (after St Clair) wears the long white coat so common in the Peninsula, and (uncommonly) shako-cords worn above the shako-cover.

47 FRANCE:
a) **Voltigeur officer, Infantry, 1812.**
b) **Grenadier officer, Infantry, 1809.**
c) **Voltigeur hornist, Infantry, 1812.**

The pre-1812 infantry coatee had cut-open white lapels, scarlet cuffs with blue flaps and scarlet collar piped white or blue. The 1810 shako (issued 1811, officially minus cords) was lower and wider-topped than the 1806 version it replaced, but its issue was haphazard and many regimental variations existed, including old-pattern plates on new caps and vice-versa, coloured lace for élites, and the continuance of shako-cords. Chinscales were worn on the later models (and sometimes earlier). The grenadiers' fur cap with brass front-plate and red plume was worn earlier in the war, causing confusion among their opponents (diarists of Fuentes de Oñoro, for example, mistake line grenadiers in fur caps for Imperial Guardsmen). Officers had gilt buttons and gold epaulettes: colonel two epaulettes with heavy fringe, major the same with silver straps, 'chef de bataillon' as colonel but fringe on left only, captains as 'chef' but with thin fringe, capt.-adjutant-major as captain but fringe on the right only, lieutenant as captain with a red stripe on the strap, sub-lieutenant with two red stripes. Quartermasters had two gold diagonal stripes on the lower sleeve, sergeants one and corporals two orange stripes, all on red backing.

The grenadier officer (after St Clair) wears regulation dress plus an embroidered sword-belt, and retains the bicorn often worn with the single-breasted 'surtout' favoured by officers in undress and on campaign. The voltigeur officer (after St Clair) has the gold-laced officers' shako (the pattern of lacing varied), voltigeur plume and collar; legwear and sandals are Spanish. Sidearms varied, the curved sabre favoured by élite officers in place of the straight-bladed fusilier type. Chinscale-bosses often bore an embossed grenade, hunting-horn or (for fusiliers) five-pointed star, though many variations existed; the star, in blue cloth, was used as a turnback-badge by some fusiliers.

The voltigeur hornist (after St Clair) wears company-distinctive shako-lace, cords, plume, epaulettes and collar, and apparently regimental uniform with musicians' lace added. Musicians were ordered to adopt 'Imperial livery' in 1812 – green jackets faced red with 'Imperial lace' of green and yellow woven eagle and crowned 'N' design, but its use was limited and often delayed until 1813–14, many regiments continuing to use multi-coloured dress.

48 FRANCE:
a) **Drum-Major, 2nd Légion de Réserve.**
b) **Drum-Major, 15th Line.**
c) **Drum-Major, 16th Light Infantry, 1812.**

Drum-majors traditionally wore elaborate uniforms, those illustrated after El Guil. The 2nd Légion de Réserve (which became the 121st Line in 1809) and the 15th Line both wear uniforms modified for active service by removal of head-dress-ornaments and (by the 15th) epaulettes and waistcoat. Another contemporary source shows the latter wearing the same hat, single-breasted dark blue 'surtout' with gold-edged black collar, pointed blue cuffs edged black, black piping down the front and bottom edges, red waistcoat with green hussar-braiding, gilt buttons, loose white overalls, no baldric and knapsack with green roll on top.

The 16th Light Infantry drum-major wears full dress, including coatee with square-cut lapels (not the pointed-ended light infantry style), a distinction apparently restricted to the 16th's musicians, whose green cloth shakos had upper and lower silver bands, silver eagle-plate below 'tricolor' cockade, silver chinscales, white plume and silver 'raquettes' and cords; their coatees were as illustrated but with scarlet collar- and lapel-piping, silver trefoil epaulettes on red backing, flat-topped green cuffs piped white, red cuff-flaps and white turnbacks; white waistcoats and gaiters and (in Spain) loose, buff-coloured or unbleached linen overalls. Drummers had black shakos with company lace and cords, green plumes, green light infantry jackets with green facings piped red (yellow collar for voltigeurs), white turnbacks, red cuff-flaps and white collar-lace, and 'company' epaulettes (green with red crescents for voltigeurs, etc.). This uniform was perhaps a version of Imperial livery as one source shows the 16th's drum-major in 1809 with a red coatee faced light green with green trefoil epaulettes, silver lace, busby ornamented only with a cockade, and blue trousers with red stripe.

49 FRANCE:
a) **Officer, 27th Light Infantry, 1809.**
b) **Drummer, 27th Light Infantry, 1809.**

The tactical distinction between light and line infantry was small, light troops often being used in a conventional infantry rôle. Light infantry uniforms changed from the cut-open coatee with pointed-ended lapels to a short-tailed, closed-lapel version after the 1812 regulations. The 'grenadiers' of light infantry were termed 'carabiniers', and the centre companies 'chasseurs'. All had dark blue waistcoat and breeches and dark blue cuffs with red flaps, with company distinctions: chasseurs, red collar piped white, shoulder-straps or unofficial green epaulettes with red crescents, white hunting-horn turn-back-badges, white shako-cords and plume in full dress; carabiniers as chasseurs, but red epaulettes, plume and grenade turnback-badges; voltigeurs, yellow collar (often piped red), white or yellow hunting-horn turnback-badges, epaulettes, plumes and shako-cords in combinations of yellow, green and sometimes red, and occasionally the busby illustrated (carabiniers sometimes had bearskin caps with red cords and plume). Officers had silver epaulettes (and sometimes short boots as illustrated); N.C.O.s had silver woven into shako-cords and epaulettes. Sabre-knots were usually green and red for chasseurs, red for carabiniers, and yellow, green and/or red for voltigeurs; the sabre was carried by many chasseurs (unofficially) as well as the regulation issue to élites. Cartridge-boxes bore brass devices corresponding to those of the line. Loose trousers of various colours were adopted on campaign, voltigeurs often favouring yellow seam-stripes.

The drummer (after Carl Colln) wears a typical regimental musicians' uniform. Note the use of an eagle-plate prior to the introduction of the 1812 pattern, adopted by some regiments years before official authorization. Musicians of the 27th wore the same uniform, but with white plume, white trefoil epaulettes, white lace, white-piped vertical pockets, scarlet turn-backs bearing white hunting-horns and silver-laced Hessian boots. See also *Uniforms of Waterloo*, Plate 63, and *Uniforms of the Retreat from Moscow*, Plates 14 and 16.

50 FRANCE:
a) Voltigeur, 16th Light Infantry, 1812.
b) Drum-Major, 17th Light Infantry, 1809.

The musicians' yellow uniform with czapka of the 17th Light Infantry replaced an earlier uniform of sky-blue with crimson facings, dark blue waistcoat and breeches, and shako. Musicians wore a similar uniform to the drum-major, with less-elaborate lace and crimson czapka-cords. El Guil shows a modified active service version, the drum-major with plume and czapka-cords removed (but with gilt chin-chain), the coatee minus epaulettes, a plain white waistcoat and un-laced yellow breeches.

The voltigeur – in part after El Guil – wears typical campaign dress. The shako has linen cover (frequently with attached neck-flap) and no chinscales (the older pattern of shako often retained long after official replacement). Instead of the coatee a tail-less, sleeved waistcoat is worn, only the wearer's collar indicating the company. Red piping – instead of the usual white – was unofficially adopted by the élite companies of a number of regiments, apparently including the 16th. Other concessions to active service included grey cloth cover for the cartridge-box, often bearing a stencilled hunting-horn with regimental number in the 'curl', and a handkerchief doubling as a neck-guard.

51 FRANCE:
Officers, Chasseurs de Montagne

The Chasseurs de Montagne originated with thirty-four companies of mountain troops raised in August 1808 to patrol the Pyrenees. The rank and file were drawn principally from the National Guard of the Departments l'Ariège, Hautes-Pyrénées, Basses-Pyrénées, Pyrénées-Orientales and Haute-Garonne, but the inhabitants were independently-minded and recruitment was difficult. Instead of the eight planned battalions, only three were organized, comprising (in 1810) 4,465 men and 161 officers, the latter mostly ex-regulars, returned *émigrés* and students. The 1st Battn was based on three companies from Dept Hautes-Pyrénées, two from Haute-Garonne and one from Pyrénées-Orientales; the 2nd from l'Ariège and 3rd from Basses-Pyrénées. Active service was limited to anti-guerrilla operations, though some of the 3rd participated in the defence of San Sebastian. Desertion was rife, General Wouillemont losing three-quarters of his 3,000 Chasseurs in an expedition into Spain in 1808–09. Disbanded in 1813–14, many of the Chasseurs transferred into the 116th Line and 4th and 25th Light Infantry.

Their infantry-style uniform perpetuated the brown colouring of the local volunteers of 1793. Other ranks wore the shako with diamond- or eagle-plate; sky-blue facings, the collar shown red or brown piped sky-blue in some cases; brown lapels with sky-blue piping are also shown. The striking full dress uniform is after Benigni, the others after drawings by El Guil, showing service dress. El Guil shows a drum-major with a light infantry-style all-brown coatee with silver buttons and chevrons on the forearms, brown waistcoat, loose white trousers, striped stockings and czapka covered with a black 'waterproof'; and other ranks with covered shako, grey greatcoat, brown breeches tucked into white gaiters and cartridge-box covered with white linen, one wearing a brown 'bonnet de police' with sky-blue piping and red tassel, brown coatee with red collar and epaulettes, sky-blue cuffs and lapels, white waistcoat and overalls; Benigni shows a private in brown coatee with sky-blue collar, cuffs and lapel-piping, brown breeches with sky-blue trefoil on the thigh, red shako-plume, black gaiters and brown rolled overcoat. Probably there was little 'uniformity': in March 1809, for example, General Wouillemont requested 'at least the greatcoats and shakos absolutely indispensable to cover the tattered country clothes of three-quarters of my men ...'

52 FRANCE:
a) Voltigeur, 2nd Paris Municipal Guard, 1808.
b) Fusilier officer, 2nd Paris Municipal Guard, 1809.
c) Grenadier, 1st Paris Municipal Guard, 1808.

Raised as a security force in October 1802, part of the Paris Municipal Guard served at Friedland; comprising two battalions, elements of both entered Spain with Murat, some 700 out of 1,162 dying in captivity after Baylen. In June 1808 a new detachment arrived in Spain to participate in anti-guerrilla operations, including a famous action at Aguilar de Campo (1811) when

Capt. Leblanc's small detachment successfully defended the local church against hundreds of guerrillas. The Paris Guard helped in the defence of Burgos in September–October 1812.

The original infantry-style uniform was green with red facings, white piping and red or white turnbacks for the 1st Battn and red with green facings for the 2nd. Contemporary sources show cuff-flaps of either the facing-colour or uniform-colour. Fusiliers had shoulder-straps of the uniform-colour, piped in the facing, and shako with brass diamond-plate, white cords and pompom of infantry company-colours. Grenadiers wore bearskin caps with brass plate bearing embossed grenade, red plume, white cords, red turnback-grenades and epaulettes, and the shako with red plume and cords on campaign. Voltigeurs had the bearskin cap minus plate, with green or white cords, green or yellow-over-green plume, green-and-yellow epaulettes, yellow collar and hunting-horns on the turnbacks, and the shako with green cords, plume and (shown by one source) upper lace band. Officers had gold epaulettes and (after Weiland) white-over-red plumes. Buttons were yellow, bearing GARDE DE PARIS and the regimental number below.

The second detachment wore white, the 1st Battn with green facings and white cuff-flaps and the 2nd with red facings. Fusiliers had white shoulder-straps piped in the facing-colour and white sailing-ships on the turnbacks, grenadiers red epaulettes and white turnback-grenades, and voltigeurs yellow collar, white hunting-horn turnback-badges, and green epaulettes with yellow 'crescents' for the 1st and red for the 2nd. Head-dress as before, with cords usually removed on campaign, when white overalls were worn. Possibly some members of the 2nd wore the white uniform at Baylen.

Musicians initially wore ordinary uniforms with gold-laced collar, cuffs and lapels, or reversed colours; with the white uniform, drummers' lace of green with yellow intersecting zigzags was worn on the collar and in six inverted sleeve-chevrons. Musicians wore ordinary uniform with gold-laced collar and gold trefoil epaulettes, the drum-major with laced lapels and pockets, and white breeches with gold stripe and thigh-knot, with a scarlet combined sword-belt and baldric, edged gold and bearing a gilt oval plate. Gold-laced bicorns, and busbies listed in an inventory of 1813, were worn by the band.

53 FRANCE:
   a) **Trooper, Lanciers-Gendarmes, Gendarmerie d'Espagne, 1811.**
   b) **Trooper, Gendarmes à Cheval, Gendarmerie d'Espagne, 1811.**

In order to protect lines of communication and establish isolated blockhouses through northern Spain, five squadrons of 'gendarmerie', each of seven officers, 80 cavalry and 120 infantry were authorized in January 1810. In June a 'legion' of 1,400 gendarmes was raised for Catalonia, and by December 1812 six legions existed, the 1st at Burgos (where the mounted units had been concentrated in November 1810), 2nd Saragossa, 3rd Pamplona, 4th Vittoria, 5th Burgos and 6th Catalonia, totalling 20 squadrons; all members were veterans from cavalry and line regiments, explaining their high calibre. In many small actions, 27 officers and 804 other ranks were killed and 86 and 992 wounded. The Burgos Legion was particularly distinguished by charging Anson's British brigade at Villodrogo (23 October 1812), their Colonel Beteille receiving no less than twelve sabre-wounds.

Both mounted and foot gendarmes wore the bicorn, and dark blue coatee with red facings and white cuff-flaps, 'chamois' waistcoat and breeches (the foot with long black gaiters, the mounted with long boots); red epaulettes for the foot (mixed with silver for N.C.O.s) and white trefoils with aiguillette on the left for the mounted; blue grenade turnback-badges. The mounted were armed as cavalry, and the foot as infantry with black leather cartridge-box bearing brass grenade-badge, and sabre with red knot. Belts were buff-leather with white edging. The mounted branch used white-laced holster-caps as well as the sheepskin. Other features used on campaign included red epaulettes for some mounted gendarmes and brown local cloth to repair or replace uniforms. Officers had silver epaulettes and buttons; musicians wore ordinary dress with silver-laced collar, cuffs and lapels.

From the end of 1810 'Chevau-Légers-Lanciers' (gendarmes with lances) were increasingly incorporated in the legions; their uniform included trefoils and aiguillette or blue shoulder-straps piped red; some sources show the shako minus white lace band, light cavalry-style coatee with pointed cuffs minus turnback-badges, braided waistcoat and buff breeches with mixed white-and-blue trefoils on the thighs. The pointed-ended blue shabraque had white lace edging and white grenades in the rear corners. Trumpeters had white-plumed shako with red ball-pompom and white cords, all-red coatee with white piping and epaulettes, white-braided blue waistcoat, red trumpet-cords, and shabraque with a double lace band. Officers often wore ordinary Gendarme à Cheval costume with bicorn. The buttons of all bore the Imperial eagle and inscription GENDARMERIE IMPERIAL/ARMÉE D'ESPAGNE.

Gendarme uniform was easily confused with that of Spanish cavalry, Marbot almost being captured by mistaking Spaniards for his own gendarmes. In December 1808 Napoleon suggested that Gendarmes detached from the Guard 'should be distinguished from the Spaniards by some peculiarity of uniform, such as a white strip on the arm'.

54 FRANCE:
  a) **Sergeant-Major, Régiment de Westphalie, 1808.**
  b) **Officer, Régiment de Prusse, 1808.**

The Régt de Westphalie was a light infantry corps formed in 1806 as a 'foreign regiment' of the French army; recruited from ex-Prussian and Brunswick soldiers, its four battalions each had six companies of 150 men each. Reduced to two battalions in October 1807, the 1st Battn (690 strong) served in Moncey's Corps in Spain; when the 2nd Battn was reduced the 1st took the title 'Bataillon de Westphalie' until incorporated in the Hanoverian Legion in September 1809. Apparently a wide variety of Prussian, Hanoverian, Saxon and Hessian uniforms and equipment were used initially, until the uniform illustrated became standard. The sergeant-major (who carried the colour on parade) wears the French 1806-pattern shako with chasseur distinctions; the heavy-bladed sabre and shoulder-belt with holster are Prussian. The colour, of regulation French design, bore on one side the inscription: L'EMPEREUR/DES FRANCAIS,/AU REGIMENT/DE WESTPHALIE and on the reverse VALEUR/ET DISCIPLINE/IER BATAILLON. The flag was almost three times the size of the French line pattern, a singular distinction; it had a spear-head, not an 'Eagle'.

The Régt de Prusse was raised in four battalions from Prussian prisoners-of-war in November 1806, becoming the 4th Foreign Regt in 1811. The original Prussian-style uniform illustrated was probably used until at least 1808. Other ranks wore French company distinctions, Prussian shakos with French diamond-plate, and 'holly-green' uniform faced scarlet. Voltigeurs had yellow aiguillettes, shako-cords, plume and sword-knot; grenadiers red cords, plume and sword-knot, and fusiliers white. Gaiters had tassel and edging of red, green or white accordingly, and grenadiers' shako-plates bore grenade badges. Musicians wore bicorns and red uniforms faced green, with gold or yellow lace; drummers wore white faced red, with red lace and (from one source) mixed red-and-white shako-cords and white plume. Drawings made in Madrid in 1808 show the closed-lapels still in use; a field officer wears bicorn with white feather, silver lace and gold tassels, gold epaulettes, white waistcoat and breeches; a company officer wears French shako with diamond-plate, gold lace upper band and cords, green plume and breeches and black sword-belt; other ranks have the shako with 'company' distinctions (e.g. voltigeur with yellow-tipped green plume, yellow cords, etc.) and brown rolled greatcoats. Musicians as above, drummers with white wings edged red and red-and-white fringe, facings edged yellow, red-and-white arm-chevrons and striped drum-hoops. A French light infantry uniform was adopted later, green with red facings, pointed-ended lapels, green waistcoat and breeches, white shako-cords (gold for officers), and plumes red (grenadiers), green (fusiliers), green with yellow tip and ball-pompom (voltigeurs); epaulettes red (grenadiers), green with yellow crescent (voltigeurs) and green shoulder-straps for fusiliers.

55 FRANCE:
a) **Pioneer, 3rd Swiss Regt, 1808.**
b) **Chef de Bataillon, Bataillon Valaison, 1808.**
c) **Voltigeur, Régt Irlandaise, 1808.**

Four Swiss regiments of magnificent standard were raised for service in the French army, wearing French-pattern uniform of a madder shade (scarlet for officers), which took a violet hue after exposure to light. The 1st Regt had yellow facings piped sky-blue, 2nd royal blue piped yellow, 3rd black piped white, and 4th sky-blue piped black. Company distinctions were French, except for grenadier epaulettes, the usual red not being distinctive against the uniform-colour; the 2nd Regt initially adopted blue and the 3rd white, the latter eventually adopted by all. The pioneer illustrated wears typical uniform, including grenadier cap, crossed-axes badges, and apron; many line and light infantry regiments dressed their pioneers as exotically as musicians. See also *Uniforms of the Napoleonic Wars*, Plate 76, and *Uniforms of the Retreat from Moscow*, Plate 28.

Other Swiss units included the Neuchâtel Battn, dressed in yellow faced red and including artillery, engineers and train detachments (see *Uniforms of the Retreat from Moscow*, Plate 15, and *Uniforms of the Napoleonic Wars*, Plates 56/57); another was the Valaison Battn, raised by the Republic of Valais in 1805 and incorporated in the French 11th Light Infantry in 1811. They wore scarlet with white facings; fusiliers green pompom, white shako-cords, red shoulder-straps piped white; grenadiers red shako-lace, cords and plume, white epaulettes and yellow grenade collar-badge; voltigeurs yellow shako-lace and cords, yellow-over-green plume, red epaulettes with yellow crescent and green fringe. Drummers wore blue faced white, six green-and-yellow lace chevrons on the arm, and company epaulettes (yellow-laced scarlet wings for fusiliers). The field officer illustrated wears the white plume of his rank.

An 'Irish Legion' was raised for French service in 1803, becoming the Régt Irlandaise in 1805, subsequently of five battalions, the first two wholly Irish in composition; in 1811 it became the 3rd Foreign Regt. The light infantry uniform, green with yellow facings, had French company distinctions (including red grenades and hunting-horns on the turnbacks for grenadiers and voltigeurs respectively), the uniform illustrated after the Carl Colln. Hamilton Smith (1813) shows a similar uniform with pointed yellow cuffs, no epaulettes, black leather belts and plain black shako with brass diamond-plate and green pompom. In addition to Irish fugitives after the 1798 Rebellion, the unit contained some British army deserters. In 1810 Sergeant Nicol of the 92nd, a prisoner-of-war, saw 'many British soldiers who had volunteered into the French service' and a Capt. Hussey from Sligo, who had been 'out with the "Boys"' in '98. Later Nicol's party was visited by 'those harpies of the Irish Brigade, Captain Reilly and Sergeant-Major Dwyer', who tried to enlist prisoners with bribes of brandy; three volunteered. Such turncoats usually met with 'no quarter' from their erstwhile comrades.

56 **SPAIN:**
   a) **Grenadier, Royal Guard, 1812.**
   BERG:
   b) **Officer, Gardes du Corps Squadron, Chevau-Légers, 1808.**

Raised as the Chevau-Légers de Berg in May 1807 by Murat (then Grand Duke of Berg), the unit's first squadron (known as the Gardes du Corps) and another company accompanied him to Spain, was incorporated in the French Imperial Guard in November 1808 and disbanded in 1809. A reconstituted Chasseurs à Cheval de Berg became the Lanciers de Berg in December

1809, served in anti-guerrilla operations, Fuentes de Oñoro and Villadrogo, and became the 1st Chevau-Légers in 1812 when a 2nd Regt was formed in Germany. The uniform of the re-established unit is shown in Black-and-White Plate 'E'; see also *Uniforms of the Retreat from Moscow*, Plate 40. The original unit wore a white 'lancer' uniform with 'amaranth' facings, the white lace and loops (silver for officers) distinguishing the Gardes du Corps squadron. Martinet shows the aiguillette and two epaulettes, with czapka minus plate, the latter probably reserved for the Gardes du Corps. Shabraques were 'amaranth', pointed-ended, with wide white lace edging (two silver bands for officers), with Imperial eagles probably added to the rear corners when incorporated in the Guard. Campaign dress (worn in Spain) consisted of czapka with black cover, grey jacket and grey overalls. Trumpeters wore 'amaranth' jacket with white facings and silver lace, and white-over-amaranth plume. The original unit was not armed with lances.

King Joseph's Guard consisted of Grenadiers, Tirailleurs and Fusiliers, many drawn from the French army, and Hussars, Artillery and Gardes d'Honneur of Spanish composition. Apparently their uniforms were like those of the French Guard, with red-and-yellow cockade. Shortages of uniform and equipment probably resulted in haphazard appearance; certainly in December 1808 Napoleon ordered '400 white coats, trowsers, &c., to be collected ... for the recruits of the royal guard. They may be taken immediately, and the recruits dressed in them, to give the guard ... a good appearance'. The Guard Hussars wore black busby with yellow-laced red bag, yellow-over-red plume, red dolman and pelisse with sky-blue facings, yellow braid and black fur, and yellow-laced white breeches.

57 KINGDOM OF NAPLES:
a) Officer, 2nd Chasseurs à Cheval, 1813.
b) Trumpeter, 1st Chasseurs à Cheval, 1811.

Committed to the war by their King (Murat), the Neapolitan units were raised principally from criminals and impressed radicals; their abysmal desertion record culminated in a suggestion that the 2nd Line should be disarmed so that when they deserted at least their weapons would be saved! In February 1808 the 2nd Chasseurs à Cheval consisted of 10 officers, 137 mounted men and 250 dismounted, reduced to 257 men by August 1809; the 1st Chasseurs arrived in Spain in February 1810. By April 1812 both were so depleted that they were reorganized at squadron strength; though never heavily engaged, by 1813 the cavalry had faded away, the remnants among the 276 Neapolitans interned by the French upon Murat's defection.

Initially the 1st Chasseurs wore a red-faced green dolman with yellow braid, red breeches and a shako; by 1808 the long-tailed dark green coatee with red facings and piping and cut-open lapels exposing white-braided red waistcoat was in use, the 2nd having a similar uniform with yellow facings and piping, white hunting-horn turnback-badges, white-braided green breeches, white metal shako-fittings, white cords and yellow-over-black plume. By about September 1809 short jackets with facing-coloured lapels were in use, trumpeters having 'reversed colours' as illustrated. By 1812 many had the single-breasted 'surtout' with facing-coloured piping, facing-coloured overalls with double green stripe and black imitation boots for service dress. The 1st at least had a 'surtout' with facing-coloured collar with pointed-ended green patch. Plumes and shako-cords were removed on campaign. Officers wore silver-laced shakos; élite companies had the busby, the Sub-Lieutenant illustrated distinguished by a single epaulette bearing a crimson diamond on the strap. The full-dress plume was green with facing-coloured tip, or crimson for élites. The contemporary print from which the officer is taken also exists with green busby-bag and green overalls with yellow stripes; some sources show officers' shabraques with a hunting-horn in the rear corners, troopers having white sheepskin (black for trumpeters) with facing-coloured 'wolf-tooth' edging.

58 KINGDOM OF NAPLES:
  a) **Fusilier captain, 8th Line, 1812.**
  b) **Fusilier, 1st Line, 1808.**
  c) **Carabinier, 1st Light Infantry, 1811.**

The Neapolitan infantry (conscripts and criminals) was even worse than the cavalry. The 1st Line arrived in Spain in 1808 1,850 strong, the 2nd in August 1808, losing 250 deserters in three days of September. Losing men at Gerona, the combined strength of both units was only 400 by September 1809. Early in 1810 the 1st Light Infantry brought 1,000 convicts into Spain as reinforcements for the 1st Line, but half deserted before they reached the Pyrenees; the 1st Light Infantry itself lost 148 deserters in June 1810 and 130 in July. Despite the efforts of the officers and a handful of reliable troops, and the recruitment of Neapolitan deserters from the Spanish army, the two line regiments were amalgamated in December 1811 into a new 8th Line, which itself dwindled to one under-strength battalion.

The original 1806-pattern French-style uniform was white with dark blue facings (white collar piped blue for the 2nd); fusiliers had blue-piped white shoulder-straps, voltigeurs yellow collars and green epaulettes with yellow crescents, and grenadiers red epaulettes and black bearskin caps with brass plate bearing a grenade, red plume and cords in full dress; the bicorn with company-coloured pompom was worn by all others. The exact shade of facing-colour is uncertain, the 'Moniteur Neapolitan' in May 1807 giving sky-blue facings for the 1st — perhaps the original colour, faded? In September 1809 a short coatee and shako were introduced, issued from French stores, though some wretchedly-equipped members of the 1st Line were reported in July 1810 minus arms and wearing undress caps and ragged trousers. In 1810-11 both line regiments were ordered to adopt scarlet facings, but the 1st retained blue. The 8th Line's regulation uniform was of French 1812 pattern, with pink facings, but was probably restricted to full dress. The Light Infantry initially wore 1806-pattern dark blue uniform with red facings, changing to that illustrated when the shako was adopted; company distinctions as the line, but voltigeurs with green epaulettes. Officers had silver lace; there was probably extensive use of brown Spanish cloth for trousers, greatcoats and possibly jackets.

59 KINGDOM OF ITALY:
a) Officer, Élite Company, 2nd Dragoons, 1811.
b) Fusilier, 5th Line, 1809.

Italian infantry units had French organization and white French-style uniform with coloured facings; fusiliers had white shoulder-straps, grenadiers red epaulettes, shako-cords and plume and (for full dress) black bearskin with brass plate, red rear patch bearing white cross, and red sword-knot; voltigeurs had green 'carrot'-shaped pompom, green epaulettes and green sword-knot with white tassel. Turnback- and cartridge-box-badges were grenades or hunting-horns as appropriate. Officers had silver lace and shako-cords and French rank-markings. The shako's diamond-plate bore the Iron Crown of Lombardy over regimental number, and the design of cockade (red, white and green) sometimes varied to distinguish battalions. There is some doubt about the colouring of uniforms, the details of regiments serving in the Peninsula below after Leinhart & Humbert: 2nd Regt white collar piped red, red lapels and cuff-flaps piped white, white cuffs and turnbacks piped red; 4th Regt red collar piped white, white lapels, cuffs and turnbacks piped green, green cuff-flaps piped white; 5th Regt red collar and cuff-flaps piped white, green lapels and cuffs piped white, white turnbacks piped green; 7th Regt green collar piped white, white lapels and turnbacks piped green, and red pointed cuffs piped white. Buttons white for all except the 2nd, yellow; shoulder-straps perhaps piped red for all. See *Uniforms of the Retreat from Moscow*, Plate 45.

The 2nd Dragoons, who won distinction in a charge at Sagunto (1811) which captured 800 prisoners and routed three Spanish battalions, had French-style dragoon uniform, brass helmet with black fur turban, black horsehair mane and crowned brass letter N on the front of the turban and red-tipped black plume (removed on campaign); the élite company wore a bearskin cap, sometimes shown with peak and embossed grenade on the plate. Troopers wore crimson-piped green shoulder-straps, some sources showing brass shoulder-scales (red epaulettes for élites); green grenade turnback-badges (silver for officers). Musicians had red helmet-mane and aigrette, red-tipped white plume, and crimson coatees faced green. Overalls and uniforms of brown local cloth were worn on campaign. Officers had square-cut shabraques with silver lace edging and crowned 'N' in the rear corners, and matching holster-caps; other ranks had white shabraque-lace, no initial, and white sheepskin holster-caps with crimson 'wolf-tooth' edging.

60 WESTPHALIA:
a) Grenadier, 3rd Infantry, 1809.
SAXE-ALTENBURG:
b) Officer, Infantry, 1808.

Among the troops supplied to Napoleon by the Confederation of the Rhine was a Westphalian contingent. The infantry had white French-style uniform with red epaulettes for grenadiers, green for voltigeurs and white shoulder-straps with facing-coloured piping for fusiliers; grenadiers and voltigeurs had red grenade and green hunting-horn turnback-badges respectively. Grenadiers had bearskin caps in full dress, others having French shakos with brass diamond-plate and chinscales, Westphalian cockade and 'company' pompom – 1st company sky-blue, 2nd white, 3rd yellow, 4th green; yellow pompom with green tuft or yellow-over-green plume for voltigeurs, red pompom or plume for grenadiers. Shako-cords and sword-knots (when worn) were red, green or white accordingly; French equipment. Before 1810 coloured facings were worn, those regiments present at Gerona, for example, having: 2nd Regt dark blue, 3rd and 4th light blue; in 1810 all adopted dark blue facings, regimental distinctions being limited to the number on the buttons. In 1812 fusiliers adopted blue epaulettes with white crescents.

The Westphalian 1st Chevaulegers present at Talavera wore a black leather helmet with black crest and white metal fittings, dark green jacket with red/orange collar, cuffs, turnbacks and piping on the single-breasted front, green breeches with red/orange thigh-knots, or grey or brown overalls; officers had silver lace and epaulettes. Lances with white and blue pennons were briefly used in 1811. Desertion-rates were high, only 390 of the 1st Chevaulegers' original 500 even crossing the frontier into Spain! Despite some creditable service the Westphalian units wasted away, only one composite battalion, the cavalry and an artillery detachment existing in April 1813; in December 1813 the remnants were disarmed by the French and interned as unreliable.

Saxe-Gotha-Altenburg contributed men to the 4th Confederation Regt, composed of contingents from the Saxon Duchies. All wore French-style uniform but the 'eye-witness' sketch on which the figure is based shows the older, German pattern still in use.

61 DUCHY OF WARSAW:
a) **Grenadier N.C.O., 7th Regt, 1810.**
NASSAU:
b) **Carabinier officer, 2nd Regt, 1813.**
CONFEDERATION OF THE RHINE:
c) **Fusilier, Schwarzburg-Sonderhausen Company, 6th Confederation Regt, campaign dress, 1810.**

The 6th Confederation Regt was composed of detachments from Schwarzburg-Sonderhausen and Schwarzburg-Rudolstadt (two companies, 350 men each), Waldeck (three companies, 400 men, white uniform faced dark blue, yellow buttons, grey breeches), and Reuss (three companies, 450 men, white Austrian uniform with light blue facings and breeches, the latter with yellow stripe and thigh-knots, yellow shako-cords and red plume). The uniform illustrated (from an 'eye-witness' sketch) shows the hard wear of campaign; the shako-plume is tied on to the sabre-scabbard by the white shako-cords, a common practice. Another contemporary picture shows a fusilier in 1810 with a locally-made shako of varnished paper with brass diamond-plate and cardboard peak, (a headdress which collapsed into pulp after rain), a goatskin as a cloak, light blue trousers with dark blue patches and rags tied round the ankles instead of gaiters. A grenadier of the Schwarzburg-Rudolstadt company also pictured has a shako with brass chinscales and grey/green cover bearing a black-painted '6' on the front, scarlet epaulettes and brown trousers.

The two Nassau regiments saw extensive service, the 1st with Suchet and the 2nd at Medellin (1809) and Vittoria. In December 1813 Col. von Kruse defected to the British with his 2nd Regt and the Frankfurt Battn, whereupon the French disarmed the remaining Confederation troops, including the 1st Nassau. The grenadiers wore the busby illustrated and red epaulettes, voltigeurs green shako-cords, yellow-tipped green plume and green epaulettes with yellow crescents; the French-style shako with brass plate usually had a black waterproof cover, the four fusilier companies having sky-blue, white, yellow or green pompom and black shoulder-straps piped yellow. All wore the distinctive yellow belts, and élites yellow grenade or hunting-horn badges on the turnbacks. See *Uniforms of Waterloo*, Plate 42 and 44.

The Duchy of Warsaw supplied three regiments (4th, 7th and 9th) for service in the Peninsula, until recalled to participate in the Russian campaign; they served with their customary valour (the 4th at Talavera and its grenadiers at Albuera, for example). Although usual Polish uniform included czapka and 'kurtka' jacket, these units adopted French uniforms (and cockades) at some point; the N.C.O. illustrated wears a grenadier bearskin, other companies having the shako. Other uniforms recorded were French coatees and (for officers) the single-breasted 'surtout'. Apparently the 4th retained the czapka and dark blue kurtka with red collar piped dark blue, yellow lapels, red cuffs and blue flaps until about 1812; other sources indicate the 7th's 'French' uniform with dark blue collar, cuffs and flaps with crimson piping and lapels, the 9th having red collar piped dark blue, white lapels, red cuffs piped white and dark blue flaps. Grenadiers and voltigeurs had French distinctions, and fusiliers green, sky-blue, yellow and violet for companies 1–4 respectively. Numerous conflicting versions exist; see *Uniforms of the Retreat from Moscow*, Plate 24.

62 COBURG-SAALFELD:
a) Private, Battn Coburg-Saalfeld, 1809.
COBURG-SAALFELD:
b) Officer, Battn Coburg-Saalfeld, 1809.
LIPPE:
c) Private, Infantry, 1809.

Schaumburg-Lippe, Lippe-Detmold, Anhalt-Dessau, Anhalt-Bernburg and Anhalt-Köthen contributed detachments to form the 5th Confederation Regt. An officer of the Lippe contingent drawn in c. 1809 shows basically the uniform illustrated (also from a contemporary sketch) with bicorn hat covered with a black 'waterproof', long-tailed coatee with white turnbacks piped green, silver epaulettes (fringed only on the left), grey breeches, black knee-boots, gilt gorget with silver device, stirrup-hilted sabre with black scabbard on a white shoulder-belt with oval gilt plate bearing silver device, black pistol-holster on a strap over the left shoulder, green-covered water-bottle in brown leather case and brown rolled greatcoat over the shoulder.

The Coburg-Saalfeld Battn at Gerona are shown by a contemporary artist as illustrated, the officer with a buff-covered hat instead of a shako. Other ranks wear similar uniform, one with brown trousers tucked into black ankle-gaiters, another in blue trousers with multi-coloured patches; all have brown elbow-patches, brown greatcoat-rolls and white-covered pouches bearing stencilled 'C'. Note the white lace loops on the cuff-flap, and the wearing of sprigs of foliage behind the red-centred white cockade, a practice usually associated with the Austrian army. Sword-knots were white.

63 HESSE-DARMSTADT:
a) **Officer, Regt Graf und Erbprinz, 1810.**
b) **Gunner, Artillery, 1809.**
c) **Driver, Artillery Train, 1809.**

Hesse-Darmstadt's contribution to Confederation forces in the Peninsula was the Regt Graf und Erbprinz (two battns of six companies each) which served in twenty-eight actions including Medellin, Talavera and the defence of Badajos, where they lost 466 casualties and the remainder captured, and a half-battery of artillery. The infantry had French-style uniform including shako with white metal shield-plate bearing the Hessian rampant lion and red-centred cockade, apparently issued in 1809 or 1810, many from French stores. Before this a bicorn was worn with company-coloured pompom (as on the shako): 1st yellow, 2nd black, 3rd blue, 4th red; officers had red plumes with black tips. The jacket had yellow facings, including lapels which were buttoned back to show a yellow plastron in full dress, and red turnbacks; fusiliers had blue shoulder-straps piped yellow, grenadiers red epaulettes, shako-cords and plume, and voltigeurs green epaulettes with yellow crescents and green plumes. Officers also wore a plain blue 'surtout' with yellow collar and (from February 1809) epaulettes of French style; N.C.O. rank-markings were French and their pompoms red with white horizontal ring and red tuft. Contemporary 'campaign' sketches show the officer as illustrated (note the neck-curtain), a voltigeur with yellow cuffs with yellow-piped blue flaps, brown elbow-patches, blue overalls with yellow stripe, grey-brown shako-cover, brass chinscales and green tufted pompom, French equipment, green sword-knot and brown rolled greatcoat. A drummer wears the same, with blue wings edged yellow, brown fur drum-apron and brass drum with light blue hoops.

The gunner (from a contemporary sketch) wears a uniform minus the regulation lace lapel-loops and with unusual collar-patches; loose trousers replace the white breeches and black gaiters. An officer also sketched in the same uniform (worn prior to the adoption of the 1809 pattern) has a silver-laced hat and ankle-length single-breasted brown coat with silver epaulettes, gilt-hilted sabre with silver knot on a plain brown shoulder-belt with rectangular buckle, brown gourd on red-and-blue string, and green-checked red neckerchief; the regulation silver-and-red sash is not worn. The artillery driver is from the same source.

64 CLEVE-BERG:
a) Grenadier, Infantry, 1811.
BADEN:
b) Gunner, Artillery, 1812.

The Grand Duchy of Baden supplied their 4th Line Regt and a battery of artillery to the Confederation troops in the Peninsula. Initially the artillery (and infantry) wore the black leather helmet with black crest and brass fittings favoured by several German states, and the uniform illustrated (after a contemporary sketch); the French-style shako was adopted later. An officer also sketched wears a black bicorn with red, yellow and white cockade, single-breasted dark blue coatee with black collar and cuffs, gilt buttons and gorget, gold epaulettes, dark blue breeches, black knee-boots, brown pistol-holster on a waistbelt, crimson leather telescope-case over one shoulder, and a straight-bladed sword with gilt hilt, black scabbard, and gold knot with red-and-yellow tassel. The 4th Line fought at Medellin, Talavera and Vittoria, tried to defect but was disarmed and interned; they wore blue with white collar and cuffs, red turnbacks, yellow buttons and blue breeches.

The 1st and 2nd Cleve-Berg Infantry went to Spain in 1809, served at Gerona and lost 605 and 709 casualties out of 1,310 and 1,313 respectively between June and September 1809. The 3rd Regt went to Spain in 1810, but at the end of 1811 all except the 2nd Battn 3rd Regt returned to Germany. The French-style uniform had light blue (some sources show darker) facings; fusiliers had white shoulder-straps piped light blue, white shako-cords and light blue sword-knot; grenadiers red epaulettes and sword-knot and full dress black bearskin with red cords, plume and rear patch bearing a white cross; voltigeurs green pompom, white shako-cords, green epaulettes with red crescent and green sword-knot with red tassel. Suhr shows cuffs as illustrated, but Weiland flat-topped cuffs with flaps, perhaps styles worn by different units. The French shako had three patterns of plate, one the diamond-plate with eagle and the others oval, one bearing the lion of Berg and the other the initial J. Striped trousers, often made from ticken, were quite common in the Peninsula. Officers had gold epaulettes and shako-lace, and favoured a grey-beige 'surtout' and breeches and bicorn for service dress. See *Uniforms of the Napoleonic Wars*, Plate 67, and *Uniforms of the Retreat from Moscow*, Plate 39.

BRITAIN
A a) Officer, Italian Legion, 1812.
  b) Officer, Light Infantry, Calabrian Free Corps, 1812

SPAIN
B a) Gunner, Artillery, 1810
  b) Grenadier, Infantry, 1808.

SPAIN
C a) Private, Regt Patria, 1808.
b) Officer, Regt Santa Fée, 1808.

SPAIN
D a) Hussar, Mina's Corps, 1813.
b) Private, Regt Fernando VII, 1808.

BERG/FRANCE

E a) Berg-Trooper, Lanciers de Berg, 1812.
    b) France – Chasseur officer, Hanoverian Legion, 1810.

SPAIN
F a) Trumpeter, 7th Lancers, 1812.
   b) Grenadier, 1st (Madrid) Regt, 1811.

A BRITAIN:
a) Officer, Italian Legion, 1812.
b) Officer, Light Infantry, Calabrian Free Corps, 1812.

Calabrian Free Corps, after Goddard & Booth (see colour plate 19); probably the light infantry detachment. Brass shako-plate, green plume; scarlet jacket, yellow collar and cuffs, dark blue piping, white turnbacks, gold lace loops and epaulettes; red sash, sky-blue breeches, black belt, steel scabbard, gilt sword-hilt, gold knot.

The Italian Legion was raised in 1811–12 from Italian prisoners in England, officers either Austrian (1st Italian Regt) or other foreigners in Sicilian service, Piedmontese, Swiss and Austrian (2nd Regt), with British field officers. The Legion served in eastern Spain, losing twenty-three killed, four officers and forty-nine men wounded and twenty-eight missing at Castalla (12–13 April 1813). They wore blue single-breasted jacket with red facings, white turnbacks; grey cloth breeches with half-boots or gaiters, each soldier to receive one jacket, a pair of 'pantaloons', a pair of cloth gaiters and cotton or linen half-gaiters. Officers' rank-marking: Lt-Col. two rows of lace around the cuff, major one, captains had buttons in pairs and subalterns equidistant; 'The officers to wear caps similar to those of the men with four inch feathers', red sash, black waist-belt and crimson-and-gold sword-knot. 'It is deeply enjoined that the utmost plainness and uniformity in dress be observed' (Lord W. C. Bentinck, 13 May 1812).

B SPAIN:
a) Gunner, Artillery, 1810.
b) Grenadier, Infantry, 1808.

The gunner (after Goddard & Booth) wears the uniform noted in Plate 34; the hat and red waistcoat could be an error on the part of the original artist. The grenadier, after Suhr, shows the tall fur cap and brass match-case on the shoulder-belt.

C SPAIN:
a) Private, Regt Patria, 1808.
b) Officer, Regt Santa Fée, 1808.

Two 'junta' regiments, from a (non-contemporary) Spanish print. Regt Patria: black shako, yellow lace and cords, brass plate and chinscales, red cockade and plume; dark green coatee with red collar, shoulder-straps and cuff-flaps, yellow piping, green turnbacks, brass buttons; white waistcoat and breeches, black gaiters, white belt, black cartridge-box. Regt Santa Fée: black shako, silver lace, chinscales, plate and pompom, red cockade; dark blue waistcoat piped red, dark blue trousers, dark blue coatee with green cuffs and lapels piped red.

D SPAIN:
a) Hussar, Mina's Corps, 1813.
b) Private, Regt Fernando VII, 1808.

The 'Leales de Fernando VII' was one of the better-organized 'junta' regiments, raised in September 1808 at Talavera, at which battle they served. The uniform-colour suggests that they were probably clothed in old stocks of the regular army's pre-1805 costume. Black shako, red lace, pompom and cockade, brass chinscales and oval plate bearing F VII; lightish-blue jacket with red collar and cuffs piped white, red piping down front, dark blue shoulder-straps piped white; lightish-blue trousers, white equipment, black cartridge-box; also shown with hide knapsack with a rolled blanket in a blue-and-white striped ticken cover. A number of contemporary pictures show what may have been attempts to standardize the clothing of the larger guerrilla bands; this uniform after Dighton: white-laced black shako, medium green dolman with scarlet collar and cuffs, white lace; medium blue overalls with red stripe and black leather reinforcing, white belts and sword-knot. Dighton shows a pink neckerchief with white spots and a brown knapsack with yellow device.

E BERG:
a) **Trooper, Lanciers de Berg, 1812.**
b) **Chasseur officer, Hanoverian Legion, 1810.**

The Peninsula uniform of the Lanciers de Berg (Plate 56): 'amaranth' shako with white lace, black peak, brass plate, white metal chinscales, white plume and white cockade, with 'amaranth' centre; dark green 'surtout' with 'amaranth' collar, cuffs, turnbacks and piping, green collar-piping; green overalls, black leather reinforcing; white belts, sword-knot and gauntlets, steel scabbard, brass sabre-hilt.

The Hanoverian Legion was intended to counteract recruitment for the British K.G.L., but few Hanoverian soldiers and only three officers enlisted, the remainder of its two light infantry battalions and two cavalry squadrons composed of assorted foreigners. Disbanded in August 1811, the Legion's personnel transferred to the 127th, 128th and 129th Line, 2nd and 4th Foreign and 3rd Berg Regts. The red French-style uniform had dark blue facings and white piping, white turnbacks, waistcoat and breeches. Officers had silver shako-lace, eagle-plate, chinscales, shako-cords and epaulettes; chasseurs had green plume and epaulettes (white epaulettes for carabiniers). The cavalry apparently wore red faced yellow and shako, though officers had black busbies with red-and-white plume, and gold epaulettes. The red uniforms caused confusion in action, Marbot noting how several men were mistakenly killed by the French at Busaco. Fearing a repetition, at Fuentes de Oñoro their commander asked General Loison if the unit could wear its grey greatcoats despite a divisional order to the contrary. Loison refused; the Hanoverian Legion were attacked by both the French 66th and French artillery, thinking them British red-coats. After losing over 100 killed and many wounded, the Legion left the firing-line, whereupon the sight of their red uniform threw oncoming French units into confusion!

F SPAIN:
a) **Trumpeter, 7th Lancers, 1812.**
b) **Grenadier, 1st (Madrid) Regt, 1811.**

Joseph Bonaparte raised seven mediocre line regiments, two light infantry and two 'foreign' regiments, the Régt Joseph-Napoléon which served in Russia (see *Uniforms of the Retreat from*

Moscow, Plate 27). The line regiments (some of which may have existed only on paper or as 'cadres') wore brown French-style uniform, with facing-coloured collar, cuffs, turnbacks, lapels and shoulder-straps: 1st Regt (Madrid) white, 2nd (Toledo) light blue, 3rd (Seville) black, 4th (Soria) violet, 5th (Granada) blue, 6th (Malaga) dark blue, 7th (Cordova) red; brass buttons, white waistcoat and breeches, black gaiters, French equipment (sabres for grenadiers and N.C.O.s) and French shako with red carrot-shaped plume, yellow cords, brass chinscales and diamond-plate bearing the cypher JN. The grenadier illustrated wears red epaulettes, loose trousers and covered shako; probably many wore haphazard dress, Napoleon ordering in December 1808 that '1,200 coats and red trowsers, hats, etc.' should be provided for the Spanish foreign battalions. The 1st (Castile) and 2nd (Murcia) Light Infantry had red-piped light green facings, light green carrot-plume with red tip, brown breeches and short black gaiters with red tassel and edging.

Joseph's six heavy cavalry regiments were uniformed like the Spanish Royal cavalry but in brown coats with facing-coloured collar, lapels, cuffs and turnbacks (all edged yellow) with seven yellow loops on the lapel, yellow trefoil epaulettes, brass buttons; facings: 1st Regt red, 2nd white, 3rd light blue, 4th pink, 5th black, 6th green. The bicorn had yellow lace edging and loop, yellow-tipped red plume, red-and-yellow cockade; white breeches and waistcoat, long boots; trumpeters wore red faced yellow with yellow-over-red plume. The 7th Lancers (la Mancha) wore a brass-fitted black helmet with dark green crest and plume, brown jacket with red lapels, turnbacks and collar-patch, red-piped yellow collar and shoulder-straps, red shoulder-rolls with yellow piping, and brown overalls with yellow-piped red stripe (see *Uniforms of the Napoleonic Wars*, Plate 54); red lance-pennon with yellow central band. The Marckolsheim MS shows a trumpeter as illustrated, wearing a red-crested helmet, red plume with yellow centre, and red coatee faced yellow. Shabraques were brown with yellow lace edging with red central line; and green with yellow edging, rounded ends bearing '7' within two cyphers in the rear corners and a grenade in the front corners for the 7th.

APPENDIX I

British infantry regiments which served in the Peninsula; details from Hamilton Smith and the Army List (1815).

Regt	Facings	Lace	Officers' lace
1st (Royal Scots)	blue	square, pairs	gold
2nd (Queen's Royal)	blue	square, single	silver
3rd (East Kent) (Buffs)	buff	square, pairs	silver
4th (King's Own)	blue	bastion, single	gold
5th (Northumberland)	gosling green	bastion, single	silver
6th (1st Warwickshire)	yellow	square, pairs	silver
7th (Royal Fusiliers)	blue	square, single	gold
9th (East Norfolk)	yellow	square, pairs	silver
11th (North Devonshire)	deep green	bastion, pairs	gold
14th (Buckinghamshire) (Bedfordshire until 1809)	buff	bastion, pairs	silver
20th (East Devonshire)	pale yellow	square, pairs	silver
23rd (Royal Welsh Fusiliers)	blue	bastion, single	gold
24th (Warwickshire)	green	square, pairs	silver
26th (Cameronian)	yellow	square, pairs	silver
27th (Inniskilling)	buff	square, single	gold
28th (North Gloucestershire)	yellow	square, pairs	silver
29th (Worcestershire)	buff	square, single	gold
30th (Cambridgeshire)	pale yellow	bastion, single	silver
31st (Huntingdonshire)	buff	square, single	silver
32nd (Cornwall)	white	square, pairs	gold
34th (Cumberland)	yellow	square, pairs	silver
36th (Herefordshire)	gosling green	square, pairs	gold
37th (North Hampshire)	yellow	square, pairs	silver
38th (1st Staffordshire)	yellow	square, single	silver
39th (Dorsetshire)	pea green	square, single	gold
40th (2nd Somersetshire)	buff	square, pairs	gold

Regt	Facings	Lace	Officers' lace
42nd (Royal Highlanders)	blue	bastion, single	gold
43rd (Monmouthshire Lt Inf.)	white	square, pairs	silver
44th (East Essex)	yellow	square, single	silver
45th (Nottinghamshire)	dark green	bastion, pairs	silver
47th (Lancashire)	white	square, pairs	silver
48th (Northamptonshire)	buff	square, pairs	gold
50th (West Kent)	black	square, pairs	gold
51st (2nd Yorkshire Lt Inf.)	grass green	square, pairs	gold
52nd (Oxfordshire Lt Inf.)	buff	square, pairs	silver
53rd (Shropshire)	red	square, pairs	gold
57th (West Middlsex)	yellow	square, pairs	gold
58th (Rutlandshire)	black	square, single	gold
59th (2nd Nottinghamshire)	white	bastion, single	gold
60th (Royal American)	See Plate 13		
61st (South Gloucestershire)	buff	square, single	silver
62nd (Wiltshire)	buff	square, pairs	silver
66th (Berkshire)	gosling green	square, single	silver
68th (Durham Lt Inf.)	bottle green	square, pairs	silver
71st (Highland Lt Inf.)	buff	square, single	silver
74th (Highland)	white	square, single	gold
76th	red	square, pairs	silver
77th (East Middlesex)	yellow	square, single	silver
79th (Cameron Highlanders)	dark green	square, pairs	gold
81st	buff	square, pairs	silver
82nd (Prince of Wales's Vols)	yellow	bastion, pairs	silver
83rd	yellow	square, pairs	gold
84th (York and Lancaster)	yellow	square, pairs	silver
85th (Bucks Vols Lt Inf.)	yellow	square, pairs	silver
87th (Prince of Wales's Own Irish)	green	square, pairs	gold
88th (Connaught Rangers)	yellow	square, pairs	silver
89th	black	square, pairs	gold
91st	yellow	square, pairs	silver
92nd (Gordon Highlanders)	yellow	square, pairs	silver
94th	green	square, pairs	gold
95th (Rifles)	See Plate 12		
97th (Queen's Own)	blue	square, pairs	silver

APPENDIX II

ORDERS OF BATTLE

To supplement the brief 'Orders of Battle' listed below, reference should be made to Oman's *History of the Peninsular War*; the changes of organization in the British Army are catalogued in C. T. Atkinson's Appendix to Oman's *Wellington's Army*, and in the Portuguese army by S. G. P. Ward in the *Journal* of the Society for Army Historical Research, Vol. LIII. The Appendix to *Military Dress of the Peninsular War* (Windrow and Embleton) is also useful.

VIMIERO (21 August 1808)

BRITISH ARMY (WELLESLEY)
1st Bde (Hill): 1/5th, 1/9th, 1/38th.
2nd Bde (Ferguson): 1/36th, 1/40th, 1/71st.
3rd Bde (Nightingall): 1/29th, 1/82nd.
4th Bde (Bowes): 1/6th, 1/32nd.
5th Bde (Craufurd): 1/45th, 1/91st.
6th Bde (Fane): 1/50th, 5/60th, 4 coys 2/95th.
7th Bde (Anstruther): 2/9th, 2/43rd, 2/52nd, 2/97th.
8th Bde (Acland): 2nd, 7½ coys 1/20th, 2 coys 1/95th.
Cavalry (Taylor): Detachment 20th Light Dragoons.
Artillery: 18 guns.
TOTAL: 16,312 infantry, 240 cavalry, 226 artillery.

FRENCH ARMY (JUNOT)
Delaborde's Div.: 2nd & 4th Lt Inf., 70th & 86th Line, part 4th Swiss (total 6 battns).
Loison's Div.: 12th & 15th Lt Inf., 32nd, 58th & 82nd Line (total 5 battns).
Reserve: Four battns formed from detached grenadier coys of line battns.
Cavalry (Margaron): 1st Provisional Chasseurs, 3rd, 4th & 5th Provisional Dragoons.

Artillery: 23 or 24 guns.
TOTAL: 10,400 infantry, 1,950 cavalry, 700 artillery.

BUSACO (27 September 1810)

ALLIED ARMY (WELLINGTON)
1st Div. (Spencer): Stopford's Bde (1/2nd Guards, 1/3rd Guards, coy 5/60th); Blantyre's Bde (2/24th, 42nd, 1/61st, coy 5/60th); von Lowe's Bde (1st, 2nd, 5th & 7th K.G.L. Line, detachment K.G.L. Light Battns); Packenham's Bde (1/7th, 1/79th).
2nd Div. (Hill): Stewart's Bde (1/3rd, 2/31st, 2/48th, 2/66th, coy 5/60th); Inglis' Bde (29th, 1/48th, 1/57th, coy 5/60th); Craufurd's Bde (2/28th, 2/34th, 2/39th, coy 5/60th).
Hamilton's Portuguese Div. (att. 2nd Div.): Campbell's Bde (4th & 10th Line); Fonesca's Bde (2nd & 14th Line).
3rd Div. (Picton): Mackinnon's Bde (1/45th, 1/74th, 1/88th); Lightburne's Bde (2/5th, 2/83rd, 3 coys 5/60th); Champalimaud's Bde (9th & 21st Portuguese).
4th Div. (Cole): Campbell's Bde (2/7th, 1/11th, 2/53rd, coy 5/60th); Kemmis' Bde (3/27th, 1/40th, 97th, coy 5/60th); Collins' Bde (11th & 23rd Portuguese).
5th Div. (Leith): Barnes' Bde (3/1st, 1/9th, 2/38th); Spry's Bde (3rd & 15th Portuguese, Tomar Militia); Eben's Bde (8th Portuguese, Loyal Lusitanian Legion).
Light Div. (Craufurd): Beckwith's Bde (1/43rd, 4 coys 1/95th, 3rd Caçadores); Barclay's Bde (1/52nd, 4 coys 1/95th, 1st Caçadores).
Pack's Independent Bde: 1st & 16th Portuguese, 4th Caçadores.
Campbell's Independent Bde: 6th & 18th Portuguese, 6th Caçadores.
Coleman's Independent Bde: 7th & 19th Portuguese, 2nd Caçadores.
Cavalry: 2 sqdns 4th Dragoons.
Artillery: 60 guns.
TOTAL: 24,796 British infantry, 24,649 Portuguese; 210 cavalry; 2,250 artillery.

FRENCH ARMY OF PORTUGAL (MASSÉNA)
II CORPS (Reynier)
1st Div. (Merle): 2nd & 4th Lt Inf.; 36th Line (total 12 battns).

2nd Div. (Heudelet): 17th & 31st Lt Inf.; 47th & 70th Line (total 15 battns).
Cavalry (P. Soult): 1st Hussars, 8th Dragoons, 22nd Chasseurs, Hanoverian Chasseurs.

IV CORPS (Ney)
1st Div. (Marchand): 6th Lt Inf.; 39th, 69th & 76th Line (total 11 battns).
2nd Div. (Mermet): 25th Lt Inf.; 27th, 50th & 59th Line (total 11 battns).
3rd Div. (Loison): 32nd Lt Inf.; 26th, 66th & 82nd Line; Hanoverian Legion (total 12 battns).
Cavalry (Lamotte): 3rd Hussars, 15th Chasseurs.

VIII CORPS (Junot)
1st Div. (Clausel): 15th Lt Inf.; 19th, 22nd, 25th, 28th, 34th, 46th & 75th Line (total 11 battns).
2nd Div. (Solignac): 15th, 65th & 86th Line, Regts Prusse & Irlandaise (total 12 battns).
Cavalry (St Croix): Two sqdns each from 1st, 2nd, 4th, 9th, 14th & 26th Dragoons.
Reserve Cavalry (Montburn): 3rd, 6th, 11th, 15th & 25th Dragoons.
Artillery: 114 guns.
TOTAL: 49,809 infantry, 8,419 cavalry, 6,822 artillery; plus battn of 924 naval ratings acting as marines.

ALBUERA (16 May 1811)

ALLIED ARMY (BERESFORD)
2nd Div. (Stewart): Colborne's, Hoghton's and Abercrombie's Bdes, as Stewart's, Inglis' and Craufurd's at Busaco, with coys 5/60th detached to form Div. light corps.
4th Div. (Cole): Myer's Bde (1/7th, 2/7th, 1/23rd); Kemmis' Bde (one coy each from 2/27th, 1/40th, 97th); Harvey's Bde (11th & 23rd Portuguese, 1/Loyal Lusitanian Legion.
Hamilton's Div.: As Busaco.
Alten's Independent Bde: 1st & 2nd K.G.L. Light Battns.
Collins' Independent Bde: 5th Portuguese, 5th Caçadores.

Cavalry: De Grey's Bde (3rd Dragoon Guards, 4th Dragoons, 13th Lt Dragoons); Otway's Bde (1st & 7th Portuguese Dragoons, one sqdn each from 5th & 8th Portuguese Dragoons).
Artillery: 36 guns.
TOTAL: 8,738 British infantry, 9,131 Portuguese; 1,146 British cavalry, 849 Portuguese; 225 British artillery, 221 Portuguese.

SPANISH ARMY (BLAKE)
Vanguard (Lardizabel): Murcia, Canarias, 2nd Leon & Campomayor Regts.
3rd Div. (Ballasteros): 1st Catalonia, Barbastro, Pravia, Lena, Castropol, Cangas de Tineo, Infiesto Regts.
4th Div. (Zayas): 2nd & 4th Guards, 4th Walloon Guards, Irlanda, Patria, Toledo, Ciudad Real Regts, Legion Estranjera.
Cavalry (Loy): Santiago, Castilla Hussars, Granaderos, Esc. de Instrucion.
Artillery: 1 battery.
TOTAL: 10,815 infantry, 1,165 cavalry, 103 artillery.

SPANISH ARMY (CASTAÑOS)
Infantry Bde (C. de España): Rey, Zamora, Voluntarios de Navarra.
Cavalry Bde (Penne Villemur): Detachments from seven regts.
Artillery: 1 battery.
TOTAL: 1,778 infantry, 721 cavalry, 62 artillery.

FRENCH ARMY (SOULT)
V CORPS
1st Div. (Girard): 64th Line (3 battns), 34th, 40th & 88th Line (2 battns each).
2nd Div. (Gazan): 28th Lt Inf., 103rd Line (3 battns each), 21st Lt Inf., 100th Line (2 battns each).
Werle's Bde: 12th Lt Inf., 55th & 58th Line (3 battns each).
Godinot's Bde: 16th Lt Inf., 51st Line (3 battns each).
Grenadier Bde: Eleven coys from 45th, 63rd & 95th Line (I Corps) and 4th Polish Regt (IV Corps).
Cavalry: 2nd & 10th Hussars, 21st & 27th Chasseurs, 4th, 14th, 17th, 20th, 26th & 27th Dragoons, 1st Vistula Lancers, 4th Spanish Chasseurs.
Artillery: 50 guns (?).
TOTAL: 19,015 infantry, 4,012 cavalry, 1,233 artillery.

SALAMANCA (22 July 1812).

ALLIED ARMY (WELLINGTON)

1st Div. (Campbell): Fermor's Bde (1/2nd Guards, 1/3rd Guards, coy 5/60th); von Lowe's Bde (1st, 2nd & 5th K.G.L. Line); Wheatley's Bde (2/24th, 1/42nd, 2/58th, coy 5/60th, 1/79th).

3rd Div. (Packenham): Wallace's Bde (1/45th, 3 coys 5/60th, 74th, 1/88th); Campbell's Bde (1/5th, 2/5th, 2/83rd, 94th); Powers' Bde (9th & 21st Portuguese, 12th Caçadores).

4th Div. (Cole): Anson's Bde (3/27th, 1/40th, coy 5/60th); Ellis' Bde (1/7th, 1/23rd, 1/48th, coy Brunswick Jägers); Stubbs' Bde (11th & 23rd Portuguese, 7th Caçadores).

5th Div. (Leith): Greville's Bde (3/1st, 1/9th, 1/38th, 2/38th, coy Brunswick Jägers); Pringle's Bde (1/4th, 2/4th, 2/30th, 2/44th, coy Brunswick Jägers); Spry's Bde (3rd & 15th Portuguese, 8th Caçadores).

6th Div. (Clinton): Hulse's Bde (1/11th, 2/53rd, coy 5/60th, 1/61st); Hinde's Bde (2nd, 1/32nd, 1/36th); Rezende's Bde (8th & 12th Portuguese, 9th Caçadores).

7th Div. (Hope): Halkett's Bde (1st & 2nd K.G.L. Lt Battns, remainder Brunswick Jägers); De Bernewitz's Bde (51st, 68th, Chasseurs Britanniques); Collins' Bde (7th & 9th Portuguese, 2nd Caçadores).

Light Div. (Alten): Barnard's Bde (1/43rd, part 2/95th, 3/95th, 1st Caçadores); Vandeleur's Bde (1/52nd, 1/95th, 3rd Caçadores).

Pack's Independent Bde: as Busaco.

Bradford's Independent Bde: 13th & 14th Portuguese, 5th Caçadores.

Cavalry (Cotton): Le Marchant's Bde (3rd & 4th Dragoons, 5th Dragoon Guards); Anson's Bde (11th, 12th & 16th Lt Dragoons); Alten's Bde (14th Lt Dragoons, 1st K.G.L. Hussars); Bock's Bde (1st & 2nd K.G.L. Dragoons); D'Urban's Bde (1st & 11th Portuguese Dragoons).

Artillery: 54 British, 6 Portuguese guns.

TOTAL: 25,577 British infantry, 17,421 Portuguese; 3,543 British cavalry, 482 Portuguese; 1,186 British artillery, 114 Portuguese.

FRENCH ARMY OF PORTUGAL (MARMONT)

1st Div. (Foy): 6th Lt Inf.; 39th, 69th & 76th Line (total 8 battns).
2nd Div. (Clausel): 25th Lt Inf.; 27th, 50th & 59th Line (total 10 battns).
3rd Div. (Ferey): 31st Lt Inf.; 26th, 47th & 70th Line (total 8 battns).

4th Div. (Sarrut): 2nd & 4th Lt Inf.; 36th Line (total 7 battns).
5th Div. (Maucune): 15th, 66th, 82nd & 86th Line (total 9 battns).
6th Div. (Brennier): 17th Lt Inf., 22nd & 65th Line, Régt de Prusse (total 8 battns & 1 coy).
7th Div. (Thomieres): 1st, 62nd & 101st Line (total 8 battns).
8th Div. (Bonnet): 118th, 119th, 120th & 122nd Line (total 12 battns).
Heavy Cavalry Div. (Boyer): 2 sqdns each from 6th, 11th, 15th & 25th Dragoons.
Light Cavalry Div. (Curto): Detachments from 3rd Hussars, 22nd, 26th & 28th Chasseurs; 13th Chasseurs (5 sqdns), 14th Chasseurs (4 sqdns), Esc. de marche; total 18 sqdns).
Artillery: 78 guns.
TOTAL: 41,575 infantry, 3,390 cavalry, 5,034 artillery.

VITTORIA (21 June 1813)

ALLIED ARMY (WELLINGTON)
1st Div. (Howard): Stopford's Bde (as Busaco); Halkett's Bde (as von Lowe's, Salamanca, plus 1st & 2nd K.G.L. Lt Battns).
2nd Div. (Stewart): Cadogan's Bde (1/50th, coy 5/60th, 1/71st, 1/92nd); Byng's Bde (1/3rd, 1/57th, coy 5/60th, 1st Provisional Battn [2/31st & 2/66th]); O'Callaghan's Bde (1/28th, 1/34th, 1/39th, coy 5/60th); Ashworth's Bde (6th & 18th Portuguese, 6th Caçadores).
3rd Div. (Picton): Brisbane's Bde (1/45th, 74th, 1/88th, 3 coys 5/60th); Colville's Bde (1/5th, 2/83rd, 2/87th, 94th); Powers' Bde (9th & 21st Portuguese, 11th Caçadores).
4th Div. (Cole): Anson's Bde (3/27th, 1/40th, 1/48th, coy 5/60th, 2nd Provisional Battn [2nd & 2/53rd]); Skerrett's Bde (1/7th, 20th, 1/23rd, coy Brunswick Jägers); Stubbs' Bde (as Salamanca).
5th Div. (Oswald): Hay's Bde (as Greville's, Salamanca, minus 2/38th; Robinson's Bde (1/4th, 2/47th, 2/59th, coy Brunswick Jägers); Spry's Bde (as Salamanca).
7th Div. (Dalhousie): Barne's Bde (1/6th, 3rd Provisional Battn [2/24th, 2/58th], coy Brunswick Jägers); Grant's Bde (51st, 68th, 1/82nd, Chasseurs Britanniques); Le Cor's Bde (as Collins', Salamanca).
Light Div. (Alten): Kempt's Bde (1/43rd, 1/95th, 3/95th, 1st Caçadores); Vandeleur's Bde (1/52nd, 2/95th, 17th Portuguese, 3rd Caçadores).
Pack's Independent Bde: as Busaco.

Bradford's Independent Bde: 13th & 24th Portuguese, 5th Caçadores).
Silveira's Portuguese Div.: Da Costa's Bde (2nd & 14th Line); Campbell's Bde (4th & 10th Line, 10th Caçadores).
Morillo's Spanish Div.: total 4,500.
Longa's Spanish Bde: 5 battns.
Cavalry: Hill's Bde (1st & 2nd Life Guards, Royal Horse Guards); Ponsonby's Bde (5th Dragoon Guards, 3rd & 4th Dragoons); Anson's Bde (12th & 16th Lt Dragoons); Long's Bde (13th Lt Dragoons); Alten's & Bock's Bdes (as Salamanca); Fane's Bde (3rd Dragoon Guards, 1st Dragoons); Grant's Bde (10th, 15th & 18th Hussars); D'Urban's Bde (1st, 11th & 12th Portuguese Dragoons); Campbell's Bde (6th Portuguese Dragoons).
Artillery: 78 British, 12 Portuguese guns.
TOTAL: 27,372 British infantry, 27,569 Portuguese, 6,800 Spanish; 7,424 British cavalry, 893 Portuguese; 3,000 British artillery, 300 Portuguese, 200 Spanish.

FRENCH ARMIES (JOSEPH & JOURDAN)
ARMY OF THE SOUTH (GAZAN)
1st Div. (Leval): 9th Lt Inf.; 24th, 88th & 96th Line.
3rd Div. (Villatte): 27th Lt Inf.; 63rd, 94th & 95th Line.
4th Div. (Conroux): 32nd, 43rd, 55th & 58th Line.
5th Div. 12th Lt Inf., 45th Line.
6th Div. (Darricau): 21st & 28th Lt Inf.; 100th & 103rd Line.
Soult's Cavalry Div.: 2nd Hussars; 5th, 10th & 21st Chasseurs.
Tilly's Cavalry Div.: 2nd, 4th, 14th, 17th, 26th & 27th Dragoons.
Digeon's Cavalry Div.: 5th, 12th, 16th & 21st Dragoons.
Artillery: 60 guns.

ARMY OF THE CENTRE (D'ERLON)
1st Div. (Darmagnac): 28th & 75th Line, 2nd Nassau Regt, 4th Baden Regt, Frankfurt Regt.
2nd Div. (Cassagne): 16th Lt Inf.; 8th, 51st & 54th Line.
Treillard's Cavalry Div.: 13th, 18th, 19th & 22nd Dragoons.
Avy's Cavalry Bde: 27th Chasseurs, Nassau Chasseurs.
Artillery: 30 guns.

ARMY OF PORTUGAL (REILLE)
4th Div. (Sarrut): 2nd & 4th Lt Inf.; 36th & 65th Line.

6th Div. (Lamartinière): 118th, 119th, 120th & 122nd Line.
Mermet's Cavalry Div.: 3rd Hussars; 13th, 14th, 22nd & 26th Chasseurs.
Boyer's Cavalry Div.: 6th, 11th, 15th & 26th Dragoons.
Artillery: 12 guns.

JOSEPH'S SPANISH TROOPS
Royal Guard Infantry: Grenadiers, Tirailleurs, Voltigeurs.
Royal Guard Cavalry: Hussars, Lancers.
Line Infantry: Regts Royal Etranger, Castile, Toledo.
Line Cavalry: Guadalajara Hussars, 1st & 2nd Chasseurs.
Artillery: 36 guns.
TOTAL: 45,500 French infantry, 4,500 Spanish; 10,200 French cavalry, 1,100 Spanish; 3,900 French artillery, 1,800 Spanish.

APPENDIX III

THE BATTLE OF TALAVERA

Frequent reference has been made to the many memoirs and diaries written by participants of the Peninsular War. An example is given below, a hitherto unpublished account of the Battle of Talavera, written by an anonymous sergeant of the 1st Battn 2nd (Coldstream) Guards. Whilst suffering from the usual failings of such accounts – sketchy tactical descriptions due to a limited view of the action – it combines many of the features commonly found in such accounts: graphic descriptions of what the writer saw, personal experiences in battle, the fate of the wounded and the spectacle of the aftermath of battle. The identity of officers mentioned but not named has been added.

'We took up a position in front of Talavera ... where we remained untill noon of the 27th at which time we ... took upon line in a position most admirably chosen ... the several Brigades were formed under cover of a grove of Olive trees with the exception of the left, which extended beyond & covered a hill. About 4 in the afternoon the enemy approached in three columns, & arriving within gun shot commenced the action with a tremendous cannonading of shot & shell, which tho' generally speaking was well directed did not produce much mischief; our park of artillery placed on the left made considerable havoc amongst theirs. The firing of small Arms did not begin untill dusk when the Enemy foolishly attempting to impose upon ... the left Line, that there were Spaniards were suffered to advance nearly to the summit when the light Infantry of Genl. Hills division opened a fire upon them & retreated, by this they were deceived, & pressed further on & the Line then poured several vollies into them charged & bayonetted them back again. Shortly after this a dreadful mistake occurred which involved the safety of no less than the lives of the whole of the light Infantry who had formed a chain of communication from one flank to the other in front of the Line. By a sudden impulse on the left the ranks commenced a kind of firing resembling a feu de joye, which communicated from one Battalion to the other & ran down with the rapidity of lightening, & by this our Battalion alone had one Lieut Col[1] mortally wounded & our Adjutant[2] was also wounded in three places & expired in the hands of the French ... who buried him & several other British Officers with distinguished military honours. Our company had also one man very severely wounded & was afterwards made prisoner, The 3d Regiment had one man killed on the spot. The left sections of the Lt Infantry were not more than 25 yards from the muzzles of the firelocks & I who was one of them seeing what was likely to happen ordered the whole of my section to lay down on their faces & thus probably preserved my life for that time. This happening at dusk every thing was quiet for about two hours when a Pistol fired by the enemy as a signal, a most furious attack was commenced on the hill on the left of the Line ... but continuing only about 20 minutes the enemy being repulsed, the firing ceased in that quarter & a fresh attack commenced on our right upon the Spaniards who had strengthened their front with a Brigade of 24 pounders ... With this formidable front the Spaniards might well resist any attack ... & they therefore allowed the Enemy's Infantry to come within 20 paces of the muzzles of their Guns when they commenced a tremendous firing of Cannon & small Arms, the Enemy in the mean time seemed determined to carry this point & fresh columns were led to the attack, their drums beating the charge, & their Officers animating their men with "Vive l'Impereur" &c but to no purpose, whole ranks were mowed down with the grapeshot of the Spaniards.

'Things remained quiet after this till day break when a general attack on our Line commenced which continued without interuppsion the *whole day* with varied sucess till about 4 o clock in the Afternoon, Victor attempted to break our Centre by a charge of two columns, who to give them their due advanced upon us, in as regular order, as if they had been going thru' the evolutions of a field day. This was the crisis ... the Army opposed to us had never seen the like before; for instead of waiting to receive them, our centre advanced upon them with a cheer, which struck them with a panic, they faced about, & received two vollies whilst retiring in confusion ... our Brigade advanced in order to preserve the line entire, & bringing up our right threatened to cut off the retreat of their flying columns, Marshal Ney perceiving this brought up his Infantry who were planted behind an Olive Grove ... & opened a most galling fire from the shelter of the Olive trees, this threw our Brigade into disorder & we retired rather in an irregular manner, however having regained the ground, we advanced, firm, our Brigade reformed, & poured in a couple of well directed vollies, which did great execution & they retired in turn persued by the light Companies. At this time having obtained entrance in the Olive Grove occupied by them the Skirmishers on both sides singled out their objects, & thus for 10 or 15 minutes were amusing ourselves shooting at one another as deliberately as if we had been Pigeon Shooting ... I cannot resist telling you that the object I had singled out, & myself exchanged three rounds each, the second of his, hit me slightly on the right Shoulder, & after my third he disappeared therefore I conclude he went home! In this service all advantages are taken to conceal one's self if possible, therefore where a tree or other object presents itself it is made use of as a Shelter. Shortly after this, they ... collected again in considerable numbers in the Wood & drove us out, & during this time I thought it impossible I should have escaped unhurt but Thank God so it happened. Two men & myself of the same company having staid behind the rest not hearing the Bugles sound the recall, were within 20 or 30 paces of the Enemy ere we perceived the others had gone in, therefore nothing but flight could prevent us falling into their hands, & facing about away we started & were instantly saluted with a Shower of Musketry & which was continued without intermission untill we reached our Line, nothing less than a miracle could have saved us, balls were loged in our clothes & knapsacks, yet unhurt!

'Shot & shells were not the only dangers presented to the contending armies for the intermediate space of ground between the lines was covered partly with standing corn & high stubble which from the incessant firing kept up on both sides, was set in a blaze several times during the day, & Lines of running fire half a mile in length were frequent & fatal to many a Soldier, some by their pouches blowing up in passing the fire, other Wounded unable to reach their respective Armies lying weltering in their gore with the devouring element approaching & death most horrid staring them in the face! Thus perished many & amongst the rest our Major of Brigade[3], one of the most gallant & at the same time useful Officers in his Majesty's service when in the act of rallying the Brigade after retiring in disorder, he was knocked off his horse & fell a victim to the flames before assistance could be given, towards dusk the firing slackened & the Enemy made a show of maneurveing with Cavalry in our front & we ... accordingly prepared to give them a reception. In order to ascertain ... their indication of movement myself & my file coverer were detached to the front under cover of the dark by Col Stopford to within half Pistol shot of them with orders to return in as quick as possible should they remove to the front; however this was nothing more than a feint to cover the retreat of their Artillery & Infantry & the whole had disappeared by day break.

'This was a dismal night great numbers of wounded on both sides lying on the field, their cries & groans were most piercingly grievous however at daylight all the assistance that could be, was given & parties were sent out from every Corps to collect them & bury the dead. This was a part of service by no means pleasant; mangled Carcases & broken limbs, was a Spectacle truly shocking & notwithstanding the utmost tenderness was used, the removal of the wounded occasioned the most piercing shreiks – It was my lot to go with a Corporal of the company to the general Hospital in Talavera, & I beheld what I never wish to see again – the road (about a mile) leading to the town was literally covered with wounded, & wounded Men dying whilst being carried there. Every street in the town was filled with them & absolutely impassible for no place had been prepared for their reception, & the Spaniards would not admit them into their houses, not even the Officers who had been billeted on them previous to the Action, without the interference of the Alcalde. They seemed to look upon us with a sort of admiration mingled with horror for it was incomprehensible to them how such a handful of Men could beat off ... the hitherto victorious legions of Bounaparte ... we remained on the ground untill the 3rd of August when the air became extremely offensive, & notwithstanding that parties of Spanish Peasantry had been daily employed in burying the Enemy's dead it was scarce completed when we broke up for Oropisa & latterly the smell became so offensive that the dead bodies were collected in heaps & laid on piles of faggots which being set fire to were thus consumed! Cuesta shot 13 Spaniards in front of our lines viz 12 for Cowardice & one (an Officer) tho' badly wounded & who sat in a chair for being taken in the service of the valiant King Joe.

'May God in his goodness preserve England from the horrors of a Campaign, you can have no idea of the ravages committed by a disappointed & exhausted army. I have many days counted upwards of an hundred bodies of murdered inhabitants & frenchmen lying on the roads; horses, mules, & asses innumerable Towns & Villages plundered & burnt, Vineyards, Cornfields &c distroyed instances too numerous & too shocking to relate ...'

FOOTNOTES:
(1) Lt-Col. Ross.
(2) Capt. & Adjt Bryan.
(3) Capt. Beckett.

BIBLIOGRAPHY

Due to the enormous number of books on the Peninsular War, the bibliography is restricted to standard works, and to those 'eye-witness' accounts actually mentioned in the text. A more comprehensive list of the latter can be found in Oman's *Wellington's Army*. Part I of the bibliography is concerned with the history of the war, and Part II the uniforms.

I

Anton, J., *Retrospect of a Military Life*, Edinburgh, 1841.

Barrès, J. B., *Memoirs of a Napoleonic Officer*, (ed. M. Barrès), London, 1925.
Batty, Capt. R., *The Campaigns in the Pyrenees and Southern France*, London, 1823.
Blakeney, R., *A Boy in the Peninsular War*, (ed. J. Sturgis), London, 1899.
Boger, A. J., *The Story of General Bacon*, London, 1903.
Bradford, Rev. W., *Sketches of the Country, Character and Costume in Portugal and Spain*, London, 1809.
Bragge, Capt. W., *Peninsular Portrait*, (ed. S. A. C. Cassels), Oxford, London, 1963.
Brett-James, A., *Life in Wellington's Army*, Allen & Unwin, London, 1972.

Cadell, Col. C., *Narrative of the Campaigns of the 28th Regt*, London, 1835.
Chichester, H. M., and Burges-Short, G., *Records and Badges of the British Army*, Aldershot, 1900, reprinted Muller, London, 1970.
Cook, Capt. J., *Memoirs of the Late War*, London, 1831.
Cooper, J. S., *Rough Notes of Seven Campaigns*, Carlisle, 1869.
Costello, Capt. E., *Memoirs of Edward Costello*, London, 1857, reprinted, (ed. A. Brett-James), Longmans, London, 1967.
Cowper, Col. L. I. (ed.), *The King's Own*, Oxford, 1939.

D'Urban, Sir B., *Peninsular Journal of Sir B. D'Urban*, (ed. I. J. Rousseau), 1930.
Dyneley, Lt-Gen. T., *Letters written by Lt-Gen. Dyneley*, (ed. Col. F. A. Whinyates), Royal Artillery Institution, 1896.

François, Capt. C., *From Valmy to Waterloo*, (ed. R. B. Douglas), London, 1906.
Frazer, Col. A., *Letters of Col. Augustus Frazer*, (ed. Mjr-Gen. E. Sabine), London, 1859.

Gleig, Rev. G. R., *The Subaltern*, London, 1823.
Gordon, Capt. A., *A Cavalry Officer in the Corunna Campaign*, (ed. Col. H. C. Wylly), London, 1913.
Grattan, Lt W., *Adventures with the Connaught Rangers*, London, 1847.
Green, W., *A Brief Outline of the Travels and Adventures of Wm Green*, Coventry, 1857, reprinted as *Where Duty Calls Me*, (ed. J. & D. Teague), Synjon Books, West Whickham, 1975.
Gronow, Capt. R. H., *Reminiscences and Recollections*, 1892 reprinted Bodley Head, London, 1964.

Harris, *Recollections of Rifleman Harris*, (ed. Capt. H. Curling), London, 1848, reprinted, (ed. C. Hibbert), Leo Cooper, London, 1970.
Hay, Capt. W., *Reminiscences*, ed. S.C.I., Wood, 1901.
Heathcote, Capt. R., *From Ralph Heathcote*, (ed. Countess Groben), 1907.
Hilton, Lord, *The Paget Brothers*, London, 1918.
Hope, Lieut. J., *Memoirs of an Infantry Officer*, Edinburgh, 1833.

James, C., *The Regimental Companion*, London, 1804.

Kincaid, Capt. Sir J., *Adventures in the Rifle Brigade*, London, 1830, and *Random Shots from a Rifleman*, London, 1835.

Lachouque, H. and Brown, A. S. K., *The Anatomy of Glory*, Lund Humphries, London, 1962.
Landmann, Col., *Recollections of my Military Life*, London, 1854.
Larpent, F. S., *The Private Journal of F. S. Larpent*, (ed. Sir G. Larpent), London, 1853.
Leach, Lt-Col. J., *Rough Sketches of the Life of an Old Soldier*, London, 1831.
Leith-Hay, Sir A., *A Narrative of the Peninsular War*, London, 1839.

Leslie, Maj. J. H., *Services of the Royal Regiment of Artillery in the Peninsular War*, London, 1908–12; (includes the diary of Capt. Bogue, R.H.A.).
L'Estrange, Sir G. B., *Recollections of Sir G. B. L'Estrange*, London, n.d.
Low, E. B., *With Napoleon at Waterloo*, (ed. M. Macbride), London, 1911; contains extracts from Sergts Robertson and Nicol, 92nd.
Luard, J., *Scarlet Lancer*, (ed. J. Hunt), Hart-Davis, London, 1964.

Marbot, Lt-Gen. Baron de, *The Memoirs of Baron de Marbot*, London, 1913.
Miles, A. H., *With Fife and Drum*, London, 1901; includes extracts from Lieut. Kingsmill, 88th, and *A Private Soldier*, 27th).

Napier, W. F. H., *History of the War in the Peninsula*, London, 1832–40.

Oman, Sir C. W. C., *History of the Peninsular War*, Oxford, 1902.
Oman, Sir C. W. C., *Wellington's Army*, London, 1912; reprinted Francis Edwards, London, 1968.

Parquin, C., *Charles Parquin*, (ed. B. T. Jones), Longmans, London, 1969.
Pivka, O. von, *Spanish Armies of the Napoleonic Wars*, Osprey, London, 1975.
Porter, Sir R. K., *Letters from Portugal and Spain*, London, 1809.

Ross-Lewin, Major H., *With the Thirty-Second in the Peninsula*, London, 1834, Dublin, 1904.

Schaumann, A. L. F., *On the Road with Wellington*, (ed. A. M. Ludovici), London, 1924.
Simmons, Maj.-Gen., *A British Rifle Man*, (ed. Lt-Col. W. Verner), London, 1899.
Smith, Sir H., *Autobiography of Sir Harry Smith*, (ed. G. C. Moore Smith), London, 1910.
St Clair, Maj. T. S., *A Series of Views of the ... Campaign in Spain and Portugal*, 1811.
Steevens, Lt-Col. C., *Reminiscences of My Military Life'* (ed. Lt-Col. N. Steevens), Winchester, 1878.
Stepney, Lt-Col. S. C., *Leaves from the Diary of an Officer*, London, 1854.
Surtees, W., *Twenty-five Years in the Rifle Brigade*, London, 1833.

Tomkinson, Lt-Col. W., *Diary of a Cavalry Officer*, (ed. J. Tomkinson), London, 1894.

'T.S.', *Journal of T.S. of the 71st*, Edinburgh, 1819; reprinted as *A Soldier of the 71st*, (ed. C. Hibbert), Leo Cooper, London, 1975.

Verner, Capt. W., *The Reminiscences of William Verner*, (ed. R. W. Verner), Society for Army Historical Research, London, 1965.
Verner, Col. W., *History and Campaigns of the Rifle Brigade*, Vol. II, London, 1919.

Warre, Lt-Gen. Sir W., *Letters from the Peninsula*, (ed. E. Warre), London, 1909.
Weller, J., *Wellington in the Peninsula*, Vane, London, 1962.
Wellington, Duke of, *Dispatches of F.M. The Duke of Wellington*, (ed. Lt-Col. Gurwood), London, 1837–38.
Wheatley, Lt E., *The Wheatley Diary*, (ed. C. Hibbert), Longmans, London, 1964.
Wheeler, W., *The Letters of Private Wheeler*, (ed. Capt. B. H. Liddell Hart), London, 1951.

II

Atkinson, J. A., *Picturesque Representation of the Naval, Military and Miscellaneous Costumes of Great Britain*, 1807.

Campbell, Maj. D. A., *The Dress of the Royal Artillery*, Arms & Armour Press, London, 1971.

Devaux, P., *Les Aides-de-Camp sous le 1er Empire*, Le Briquet, Orleans.

Goddard, T. and Booth, I., *Representation of the Principal European Armies*, London, 1812.

Haswell Miller, A. E. and Dawnay, N. P., *Military Drawings and Paintings in the Royal Collection*, Phaidon, London, Vol. I, 1966, Vol. II, 1970.
Haythornthwaite, P. J., Cassin-Scott, J. and Fabb, J., *Uniforms of the Napoleonic Wars*, Blandford Press, Poole, 1973.
Haythornthwaite, P. J., *Uniforms of the Retreat from Moscow*, Blandford Press, Poole, 1976.

Haythornthwaite, P. J., *Uniforms of Waterloo*, Blandford Press, Poole, 1974.

Kannik, P., *Military Uniforms of the World*, Blandford Press, Poole, 1968.

Knötel, R. & H. and Sieg, H., *Handbuch der Uniformkunde*, Hamburg, 1937, reprinted 1964.

Lachouque, H., *Dix Siècles de Costume Militaire*, Hachette, Paris, 1963.

Lawson, C. C. P., *History of the Uniforms of the British Army*, Vol. IV, Norman Military Publications, London, 1966, Vol. V, Kaye & Ward, London, 1967.

Malibron, C., *Guide à l'Usage des Artistes et Costumiers*, Paris, 1904–07; reprinted by Olmes, Krefeld, 1972.

Martin, P., *Der Bunte Rock (Military Costume)*, Jenkins, London, and Keller, Stuttgart, 1963; reprinted as *European Military Uniforms*, Spring Books, London, 1967.

Martinet, P., *Galerie Militaire–Troupes Étrangères*, Paris, c. 1810.

Quennevat, J.-C., *Les Vrais Soldats de Napoléon*, Sequoia-Elsevier, Paris, 1968.

Windrow, M. and Embleton, G., *Military Dress of the Peninsular War*, Ian Allan, London, 1974.

SERIES OF PRINTS, ETC.
'Soldats et Uniformes du Premier Empire' (Dr F. G. Hourtoulle).
'L'Armée Française' (L. Rousselot).
'Soldats d'Autrefois' (L. Rousselot).
'Le Plumet' ('Rigo').
'Les Uniformes du Premier Empire' (ed. Cmdt E. L. Bucquoy).
'Uniformenkunde' (R. Knötel).
'Heere der Vergangenheit' (J. Olmes).
'British Military Uniforms and Equipment' (Kingsland Cox Ltd, London).

PERIODICALS

Individual articles too numerous to mention in:

Journal of the Society for Army Historical Research.
Tradition (International Society of Military Collectors).

Gazette des Uniformes (Société d'Edition de Revues d'Armes).
History Today (Vol. XXVI: article by M. Glover on the Portuguese army, containing hitherto unpublished material).
Royal Military Chronicle (1812–13).
United Service Journal (1831).
London Gazette (1812–14).
The Public Ledger (1813).

ARTISTS

The following contemporary artists (among others) were consulted:

John Augustus Atkinson, J. Barwell, Capt. Robert Batty, Charles Random de Berenger, Denis Dighton, Robert Dighton Jun., 'El Guil', Thomas Heaphy, William Heath, L. von Hugo, Sir Thomas Lawrence, Pierre Martinet, John Scott, Charles Hamilton Smith, Major Thomas S. St Clair, Cornelius and Christophe Suhr, C. F. Weiland, Lieut. E. Wheatley.

Among the more modern artists consulted were:

Col. Ribeiro Arthur, R. Forthoffer, 'JOB' (J. Onfroy de Bréville), E. Leliepvre, René North, Carlos Ribeiro, 'Rigo' (A. Rigondaud), L. Rousselot.

Corunna
Galicia
Asturias
Leon
Astorga
Sahagun
Vigo
Benavente
Leon
Oporto
Douro R.
PORTUGAL
Salamanca
Almeida
Ciudad Rodrigo
Busaco
Fuentes de Onoro
Talavera
Estremadura
Rolica
Vimiero
Atlantic Ocean
Cintra
LISBON
Arroyo dos Molinos
Elvas
Guadiana R.
Setubal
Badajos
Medellin
Albuera
Guadiana R.
Guadalquivir R.
Cadiz
Barrosa
Gibraltar